The Blac

at Ticonderoga

The Black Watch at Ticonderoga

Campaigns in the French & Indian War

Frederick B. Richards

LEONAUR

The Black Watch at Ticonderoga: Campaigns in the French & Indian War
Frederick B. Richards

Published by Leonaur Ltd

Text in this form copyright © 2007 Leonaur Ltd

ISBN: 978-1-84677-286-3 (hardcover)
ISBN: 978-1-84677-285-6 (softcover)

http://www.leonaur.com

Publisher's Note

The opinions expressed in this book are those of the author
and are not necessarily those of the publisher.

Contents

Ticonderoga   7
Introduction   17
A Brief History of the Black Watch   25
The French & Indian War   32
The Ticonderoga Campaign   42
Beyond the Battle   75
Major Duncan Campbell   82
Roll of Officers of the 42nd Highlanders   89
Roll of Capt. John Reid's Company,
    November 1757   93
Roll of Capt. James Murray's Company,
    November 1757   96
Black Watch Losses at Ticonderoga Compared
    With Those of Other Wars   98
Table of Losses of Black Watch in
    Seven Year War   100
Official Titles of Black Watch at
    Different Periods   101
Principal Campaigns, Battles, Etc.   103
British Regiments at Ticonderoga1758   105
British Regiments at Ticonderoga1759   111
Provincial Regimentsat Ticonderoga   113
Biographical Sketches of Someof the
    Officers of 1758   115
Original Regimental List of the
    Black Watch   146
Officers of the 42nd Royal Highland
    Regiment   148
The Black Watch in the1759 Campaign   151

Ticonderoga

A Legend of the West Highlands

TICONDEROGA

This is the tale of the man
Who heard a word in the night
In the land of the heathery hills,
In the days of the feud and the fight.
By the sides of the rainy sea,
Where never a stranger came,
On the awful lips of the dead,
He heard the outlandish name.
It sang in his sleeping ears,
It hummed in his waking head:
The name - Ticonderoga,
The utterance of the dead.

I. THE SAYING OF THE NAME

On the loch-sides of Appin,
When the mist blew from the sea,
A Stewart stood with a Cameron:
An angry man was he.
The blood beat in his ears,
The blood ran hot to his head,
The mist blew from the sea,

And there was the Cameron dead.
"O, what have I done to my friend,
O, what have I done to mysel',
That he should be cold and dead,
And I in the danger of all?

Nothing but danger about me,
Danger behind and before,
Death at wait in the heather
In Appin and Mamore,
Hate at all of the ferries
And death at each of the fords,
Camerons priming gunlocks
And Camerons sharpening swords."

But this was a man of counsel,
This was a man of a score,
There dwelt no pawkier Stewart
In Appin or Mamore.
He looked on the blowing mist,
He looked on the awful dead,
And there came a smile on his face
And there slipped a thought in his head.

Out over cairn and moss,
Out over scrog and scaur,
He ran as runs the clansman
That bears the cross of war.
His heart beat in his body,
His hair clove to his face,
When he came at last in the gloaming
To the dead man's brother's place.
The east was white with the moon,
The west with the sun was red,

And there, in the house-doorway,
Stood the brother of the dead.

"I have slain a man to my danger,
I have slain a man to my death.
I put my soul in your hands,"
The panting Stewart saith.
"I lay it bare in your hands,
For I know your hands are leal;
And be you my targe and bulwark
From the bullet and the steel."

Then up and spoke the Cameron,
And gave him his hand again:
"There shall never a man in Scotland
Set faith in me in vain;
And whatever man you have slaughtered,
Of whatever name or line,
By my sword and yonder mountain,
I make your quarrel mine.
I bid you in to my fireside,
I share with you house and hall;
It stands upon my honour
To see you safe from all."

It fell in the time of midnight,
When the fox barked in the den
And the plaids were over the faces
In all the houses of men,
That as the living Cameron
Lay sleepless on his bed,
Out of the night and the other world,
Came in to him the dead.

"My blood is on the heather,
My bones are on the hill;
There is joy in the home of ravens
That the young shall eat their fill.
My blood is poured in the dust,
My soul is spilled in the air;
And the man that has undone me
Sleeps in my brother's care."

"I'm wae for your death, my brother,
But if all of my house were dead,
I couldnae withdraw the plighted hand,
Nor break the word once said."

"O, what shall I say to our father,
In the place to which I fare?
O, what shall I say to our mother,
Who greets to see me there?
And to all the kindly Camerons
That have lived and died long-syne -
Is this the word you send them,
Fause-hearted brother mine?"

"It's neither fear nor duty,
It's neither quick nor dead
Shall gar me withdraw the plighted hand,
Or break the word once said."

Thrice in the time of midnight,
When the fox barked in the den,
And the plaids were over the faces
In all the houses of men,
Thrice as the living Cameron
Lay sleepless on his bed,
Out of the night and the other world

Came in to him the dead,
And cried to him for vengeance
On the man that laid him low;
And thrice the living Cameron
Told the dead Cameron, no.

"Thrice have you seen me, brother,
But now shall see me no more,
Till you meet your angry fathers
Upon the farther shore.
Thrice have I spoken, and now,
Before the cock be heard,
I take my leave for ever
With the naming of a word.
It shall sing in your sleeping ears,
It shall hum in your waking head,
The name – Ticonderoga,
And the warning of the dead."

Now when the night was over
And the time of people's fears,
The Cameron walked abroad,
And the word was in his ears.
"Many a name I know,
But never a name like this;
O, where shall I find a skilly man
Shall tell me what it is?"
With many a man he counselled
Of high and low degree,
With the herdsmen on the mountains
And the fishers of the sea.
And he came and went unweary,
And read the books of yore,
And the runes that were written of old

On stones upon the moor.
And many a name he was told,
But never the name of his fears -
Never, in east or west,
The name that rang in his ears:
Names of men and of clans;
Names for the grass and the tree,
For the smallest tarn in the mountains,
The smallest reef in the sea:
Names for the high and low,
The names of the craig and the flat;
But in all the land of Scotland,
Never a name like that.

II. THE SEEKING OF THE NAME

And now there was speech in the south,
And a man of the south that was wise,
A periwig'd lord of London,
Called on the clans to rise.
And the riders rode, and the summons
Came to the western shore,
To the land of the sea and the heather,
To Appin and Mamore.
It called on all to gather
From every scrog and scaur,
That loved their fathers' tartan
And the ancient game of war.

And down the watery valley
And up the windy hill,
Once more, as in the olden,
The pipes were sounding shrill;
Again in highland sunshine

The naked steel was bright;
And the lads, once more in tartan
Went forth again to fight.

"O, why should I dwell here
With a weird upon my life,
When the clansmen shout for battle
And the war-swords clash in strife?
I cannae joy at feast,
I cannae sleep in bed,
For the wonder of the word
And the warning of the dead.
It sings in my sleeping ears,
It hums in my waking head,
The name - Ticonderoga,
The utterance of the dead.
Then up, and with the fighting men
To march away from here,
Till the cry of the great war-pipe
Shall drown it in my ear!"

Where flew King George's ensign
The plaided soldiers went:
They drew the sword in Germany,
In Flanders pitched the tent.
The bells of foreign cities
Rang far across the plain:
They passed the happy Rhine,
They drank the rapid Main.
Through Asiatic jungles
The Tartans filed their way,
And the neighing of the war-pipes
Struck terror in Cathay.

"Many a name have I heard," he thought,
"In all the tongues of men,
Full many a name both here and there.
Full many both now and then.
When I was at home in my father's house
In the land of the naked knee,
Between the eagles that fly in the lift
And the herrings that swim in the sea,
And now that I am a captain-man
With a braw cockade in my hat -
Many a name have I heard," he thought,
"But never a name like that."

III. The Place of the Name

There fell a war in a woody place,
Lay far across the sea,
A war of the march in the mirk midnight
And the shot from behind the tree,
The shaven head and the painted face,
The silent foot in the wood,
In a land of a strange, outlandish tongue
That was hard to be understood.

It fell about the gloaming
The general stood with his staff,
He stood and he looked east and west
With little mind to laugh.
"Far have I been and much have I seen,
And kent both gain and loss,
But here we have woods on every hand
And a kittle water to cross.
Far have I been and much have I seen,
But never the beat of this;

And there's one must go down to that waterside
To see how deep it is."

It fell in the dusk of the night
When unco things betide,
The skilly captain, the Cameron,
Went down to that waterside.
Canny and soft the captain went;
And a man of the woody land,
With the shaven head and the painted face,
Went down at his right hand.
It fell in the quiet night,
There was never a sound to ken;
But all of the woods to the right and the left
Lay filled with the painted men.

"Far have I been and much have I seen,
Both as a man and boy,
But never have I set forth a foot
On so perilous an employ."
It fell in the dusk of the night
When unco things betide,
That he was aware of a captain-man
Drew near to the waterside.
He was aware of his coming
Down in the gloaming alone;
And he looked in the face of the man
And lo! the face was his own.
"This is my weird," he said,
"And now I ken the worst;
For many shall fall the morn,
But I shall fall with the first.
O, you of the outland tongue,
You of the painted face,

This is the place of my death;
Can you tell me the name of the place?"
"Since the Frenchmen have been here
They have called it Sault-Marie;
But that is a name for priests,
And not for you and me.
It went by another word,"
Quoth he of the shaven head:
"It was called Ticonderoga
In the days of the great dead."

And it fell on the morrow's morning,
In the fiercest of the fight,
That the Cameron bit the dust
As he foretold at night;
And far from the hills of heather
Far from the isles of the sea,
He sleeps in the place of the name
As it was doomed to be.

Robert Louis Stevenson

Introduction

A residence of ten years in Ticonderoga inspired me with an appreciation of the history of that most historic spot in America, and when as secretary of the Ticonderoga Historical Society I was instrumental in securing the erection of the Black Watch Memorial in that village, I became particularly interested in the record of that famous Highland Regiment which this building commemorates.

It has for several years been my wish to write so complete an account of the Black Watch at Ticonderoga that one would need look in no other place for any detail in the history of that regiment from the time it left Scotland in 1756 until after the capture of Ticonderoga by Amherst in 1759.

As a meeting of the New York State Historical Association on Lake Champlain seemed an appropriate time to present such a paper and the printed histories of that period give only meagre accounts on this subject, Mrs. Richards and I made this an excuse for a trip to the British Isles and a large part of August and September, 1910, was spent on a Black Watch pilgrimage. We had a very enjoyable trip and gained many interesting facts but I am sorry to say that the story is still far from complete.

The reason for the lack of more detailed information

about the Regiment in the Ticonderoga period is found in the following which is from the preface of Stewart of Garth's first edition:

The origin of these Sketches and Military Details was simply this: When the Forty-second regiment was removed from Dublin to Donaghadee in the year 1771, the baggage was sent round by sea. The vessel having it on board was unfortunately driven on shore by a gale of wind, and wrecked; the greater part of the cargo and baggage was lost, and the portion saved, especially the regimental books and records, was much injured. A misfortune somewhat similar occurred, when the army, under the Earl of Moira, landed at Ostend in June, 1794. The transports were ordered round to Helvoetsluys, with orders to wait the further movements of the troops. But the vessels had not been long there, when the enemy invaded Holland in great force, and, entering Helvoetsluys, seized on the transports in the harbour. Among the number of vessels taken were those which had conveyed the Forty-second to Flanders, having on board every article of regimental baggage, except the knapsacks with which the officers and soldiers had landed at Ostend in light marching order. Along with the baggage, a well-selected library, and, what was more to be regretted, all that remained of the historical records of the regiment, from the period of its formation till the year 1793, fell into the hands of the enemy.

After the conclusion of the late war, his Royal Highness, the Commander-in-Chief, directed that

GRENADIER, 42ᴺᴰ REGᵀ 1751.
(From a painting at Windsor Castle.)

A GRENADIER OF THE 42ND REGIMENT, 1751

the Forty-second should draw up a record of its services and enter it in the regimental books, for the information of those who should afterwards belong to the corps. As none of the officers who had served previously to the loss of the records in 1794 were then in the regiment, some difficulty arose in drawing up the required statement of service; indeed, to do so correctly was found impossible, as, for a period of fifty-four years previous to 1793, the materials were very defective. In this situation, the commanding officer, in the year 1817, requested me to supply him with a few notices on the subject.

It seemed to have been the custom in the British army of that period for a Regiment to carry its entire belongings with it from place to place and this unfortunate practice has swept from existence every trace of the Regimental records of the Black Watch of Ticonderoga.

It may be readily seen that if Colonel Stewart who had all the information in 1817 which the British government was able to supply and who was also fortunate in having had an intimate acquaintance during his service in the Regiment with officers who have served almost from its formation, was unable to write a complete record, the task nearly one hundred years later might be considered well nigh hopeless. There was the hope, however, that some record which was then lost might have been discovered since Colonel Stewart's time or that interesting matter might be found in the archives of the families who had sons in the Black Watch of 1758. It is a fact that only recently the regimental records of the Black Watch of two decades later were found in an old second-hand bookstore in Portsmouth and it is still possible that the regimental records of 1758-9, which are now lost, may yet come to light.

We find that nearly all the histories of the Highland Regiments follow Stewart of Garth nearly word for word in their accounts of the early history of the Black Watch. A notable exception, however, is *A Military History of Perthshire*, which has much that is new. There are also many interesting letters and other records in *The Chronicles of the Atholl and Tullibardine Families*, relating to the service of those of the Black Watch who came from the Atholl family or estate, and at London we found some dispatches in the Public Record Office in the War Department which I have not seen published. The chief merit, however, if any, which I can claim for this book is that while it does not add much that is new, it does, I think, collect in one place nearly all that is known about the Black Watch of the Ticonderoga period.

I might say here, also, that whatever was lacking in information was more than made up by the cordiality of our reception, as we found nearly every Scotsman interested in the oldest Highland Regiment of the British Army and glad to help us in anyway possible.

We are under special obligation, which I here wish to acknowledge, to Lt. Col. Hugh Rose, the present commander of the First Battalion of the Black Watch; Major D. L. Wilson Farquharson, D. S. 0., who represented the Regiment at the unveiling of the memorial tablet at Ticonderoga, July 4, 1906, now retired and living in Allargue in Aberdeenshire, the home of the Farquharson's for many generations; W. Skeoch Gumming of Edinburgh, artist and authority on Scottish costumes and tartans of the 18th century; Mrs. Campbell of Dunstaffnage, present owner of old Inverawe House; the Marchioness of Tullibardine, editor of *A Military History of Perthshire*, and the Duke of Atholl, present head of the Clan Murray, Honorary Colonel of the Third Battalion of the Black Watch and compiler of the *Chronicles of the Atholl and Tullibardine Families*.

CHAPTER 1

A Brief History of
the Black Watch

Before proceeding to the Black Watch of Ticonderoga, it would perhaps be well to give a brief history of the Regiment.

There is considerable difference of opinion as to just when the independent companies which were afterwards to become the present regiment of the line were raised. The earliest record I have seen is that on the 3rd of August, 1667, King Charles II issued a commission under the Great Seal to John, second Earl of Atholl "to raise and keep such a number of men as he should think fit to be a constant guard for securing the peace in the Highlands" and "to watch upon the braes."[1]

From this time until 1739 the Black Watch was in various stages of formation.[2]

It was at the period of the independent companies that the name Black Watch was given; *Black* from the sombre tartan in contrast to the regular soldiers who at that time had coats, waistcoats and breeches of scarlet cloth,

---

1. *A Military History of Perthshire.*
2. The most complete account of the independent companies may be found in *A Military History of Perthshire.*

and *Watch* because their duties were to watch or keep order in the Highlands. The character of the rank and file of the Black Watch of this period was exceedingly high, many gentlemen with servants serving as privates, and in addition to the enlistment being from the best families it was also possible to select only "men of full height, well proportioned and of handsome appearance."

There were several reasons for this, the principal one being probably the fact that at that period the carrying of arms was prohibited by penalties and it became an "object of ambition with all the young men of spirit to be admitted even as privates into a service which gave them the privilege of wearing arms." Our interest in the Black Watch, however, is principally in the Regiment of the line as such and this dates from the commission given by George II, October 25, 1739, as follows:

George R.

Whereas we have thought fit, that a regiment of foot be forthwith formed under your command, and to consist of ten companies, each to contain one captain, one lieutenant, one ensign, three sergeants, three corporals, two drummers, and one hundred effective private men; which said regiment shall be partly formed out of six Independent Companies of Foot[2] in the Highlands of North Britain, three of which are now commanded by captains, and three by captain-lieutenants. Our will and pleasure therefore is, that one sergeant, one corporal, and fifty private men, be forthwith taken out of the three companies commanded by captains, and ten private men from the three commanded by captain-lieutenants,

The Method of Wearing the Belted Plaid

making one hundred and eighty men, who are to be equally distributed into the four companies hereby to be raised; and the three sergeants and three corporals, draughted as aforesaid, to be placed to such of the four companies as you shall judge proper; and the remainder of the non-commissioned officers and private men, wanting to complete them to the above number, to be raised in the Highlands with all possible speed; the men to be natives of that country, and none other to be taken.

This regiment shall commence and take place according to the establishment thereof. And of these our orders and commands, you, and the said three captains, and the three captain-lieutenants commanding at present the six Independent Highland Companies, and all others concerned, are to take notice, and to yield obedience thereunto accordingly.

Given at our Court at St. James's, this 25th day of October, 1739, and in the 13th year of our reign.

By His Majesty's Command,

(Signed): *Wm. Yonge*

To our Right Trusty and Right Well Beloved Cousin, John Earl of Craufurd and Lindsay.

May, 1740, these ten companies were mustered in a field between Taybridge and Aberfeldy and in the army list of that year were known as "Earl of Crawford's Regiment of Foot in the Highlands." There have been several changes of the official name of the Regiment but the "Black Watch" was always the familiar one in the country where it has drawn its recruits and since 1881 has been the official name in the British Army List.

The uniform of this period was a "scarlet jacket and waistcoat, with buff facings and white lace, tartan plaid of twelve yards plaited round the middle of the body, the upper part being fixed on the left shoulder, ready to be thrown loose and wrapped over both shoulders and firelock in rainy weather. At night, the plaid served the purpose of a blanket, and was a sufficient covering for the Highlanders. These were called belted plaids, from being kept tight to the body by a belt, and were worn on guards, reviews, and on all occasions when the men were in full dress. On this belt hung the pistols and dirk when worn. In the barracks, and when not on duty, the little kilt or *philibeg* was worn, a blue bonnet with a border of white, red, and green, arranged in small squares to resemble, as is said, the fess cheque in the arms of the different branches of the Stewart family, and a tuft of feathers, or sometimes, from economy or necessity, a small piece of black bearskin. The arms were a musket, a bayonet, and a large baskethilted broadsword. These were furnished by Government; such of the men as chose to supply themselves with pistols and dirks were allowed to carry them, and targets after the fashion of the country. The sword-belt was of black leather, and the cartouch-box was carried in front, supported by a narrow belt round the middle."[1]

"While the companies acted independently, each commander assumed the tartan of his own Clan. When embodied, no clan having a superior claim to offer an uniform plaid to the whole, and Lord Crawford, the colonel, being a Lowlander, a new pattern was assumed, and which has ever since been known as the 42nd, or Black Watch

---

1. Stewart of Garth, Page 246, Vol. I.

tartan, being distinct from all others.[1] Lord John Murray gave the Athole tartan for the *philibeg*. The difference was only a stripe of scarlet, to distinguish it from that of the belted plaid. The pipers wore a red tartan of very bright colours, (of the pattern known by the name of the Stewart or Royal Tartan), so that they could be more clearly seen at a distance. When a band of music was added, plaids of the pipers' pattern were given to them."[2]

---

1. Capt. I. H. Mackay Scobie claims that this tartan was probably evolved from a Campbell Sett and was a Government pattern for Government service, worn by the independent companies of the Black Watch before embodied in 1739 and also by other Scottish regiments. "The Government or Black Watch Tartan" Army Historical Research, Vol. I, Page 154.
2. Stewart of Garth, Page 247, Vol. I.

CHAPTER 2

The French & Indian War

Having given briefly the origin of the Regiment, we will pass to the period which is the subject of this book.

May, 1756, war having been formally declared between France and England, a body of troops, the Highlanders forming a part, were embarked under the command of Lieut. General James Abercrombie and landed at New York, June, 1756. These were soon followed by more troops under the Earl of Loudon who was appointed Commander-in-Chief of the Army of America.

The official name of the Regiment at this time was the 42nd Regiment of Foot, but they are often spoken of in dispatches simply as the Highlanders, because they were the only Highland Regiment then in this section, or as Lord John Murray's Highlanders from the custom of the times of calling a Regiment by the name of its Honorary Colonel. The commander of the Black Watch at this time was Lieut. Col. Francis Grant, son of the Laird of Grant, who had served in the Regiment from the time he had received his commission as Ensign, October 25, 1739. He was made Lieutenant Colonel December 17, 1755 and was in command of the Regiment all through the American campaign. The only other officer who had served continuously from the formation of the Regiment in 1739 was Gordon Graham of Drainie, who in 1756 was senior captain.

The record of the Regiment from the landing in June, 1756, until the battle of July, 1758, is exceedingly meagre. In fact nothing of importance was done by the whole army. As one author puts it "Loudon was so engrossed in schemes for improving the condition of his men that he seemed to have no time for employing them against the enemy." The following extract from a letter from the Earl of Loudon to William Pitt dated New York, March 10th, 1757, will illustrate the method of quartering troops of that period.

In the end of your letter you have acquainted me, that words shall be inserted, in the mutiny act to take away every doubt about the Right of Quartering extending to America.

When I writ on that subject, I was but just arrived, and the troops were mostly encamped. Since that I have had disputes to settle, all over this Continent, in settling the winter quarters for the Troops from whence I find, that the manner of quartering in England, as in time of peace, on Publick Houses only, will in no shape answer the intent in this country, for there are few Publick Houses and most of them sell nothing but spirits, where they possess only one room in which they sell the liquor, where men cannot be quartered.

Whilst the war lasts, necessity will justify exceeding that rule, as Troops must be under cover, in the places where it is necessary to post them, for the security of the country and carrying on the service, but as soon as a peace comes, it will, by the English rule, be impossible to quarter any number of Troops, in this country, without a new regulation, and the only remedy that occurs to me at present, is adopting the method of quartering in Scotland, where for the same reason of there not being Publick Houses sufficient for the reception of Troops they are by law quartered on private houses.

I must beg leave to give you one instance of the situation of quarters here. When I arrived at Albany, I do not believe it was possible to have quartered Fifty men on that town, on all the Publick Houses in it, and taking a full survey of it, I found that by quartering on the Private Houses, I can, without incommoding them, in the parts of their houses, in which they live, quarter Fourteen Hundred men, and for a short time, in case of necessity, I could quarter Two thousand. I have mentioned this to show you what the situation of all the Frontier Places, in this country that are liable to attacks, must be, if quartering is likely to be kept to, on Publick Houses only.

On the 10th instant arrived the Harriet Packet which brought me the duplicates of your letters of the 9th and 11th of January, and the next day came in here His Majesty's ship the Hampshire commanded by Captain Norbury, having under his convoy the nine additional companies of the Highlanders, who had a passage of twelve weeks from Cork, and met with very bad weather; of this convoy there were missing on his arrival in this Port, the Arundal and Salisbury Transports. The last we have, since, accounts of her getting into Rhode Island.

The Troops being sickly, I have cantoned them in villages adjacent to this Port, for the sake of fresh provisions and vegetables.

In the published histories of the time it is stated that the "42nd remained inactive in or near Albany during 1756 and that throughout the winter and spring of the following year the men were drilled and disciplined for bush fighting and marksmanship, a species of warfare for which they were well fitted, being for the most part good shots and experts in the management of arms."

From the following letters found in the Public Record Office in London the quarters for the winter of 1756-7 were probably at Schenectady. Extract from letter from Loudon to Pitt, New York, 25th April, 1757, "The Highlanders were set in motion from Schenectady. . . . they marched without tents and lay in the woods upon the snow making great fires and I do not find the troops have suffered. . . . We have on that River (Mohawk) at Schenectady and up to the German Flats, the Highland Regiment upwards of a thousand men," etc.

The second letter reads as follows, and while it is chiefly of interest in this connection because it is dated from Schenectady, it also illustrates the custom of selling commissions:

Schenectady
April 24, 1757
Francis Grant, Lt. Col. 42nd Regiment
Sir, I am convinced from several things that have happened me since I have been in the Regiment that my continuing to serve any longer in it would be disagreeable to the whole corps of officers and

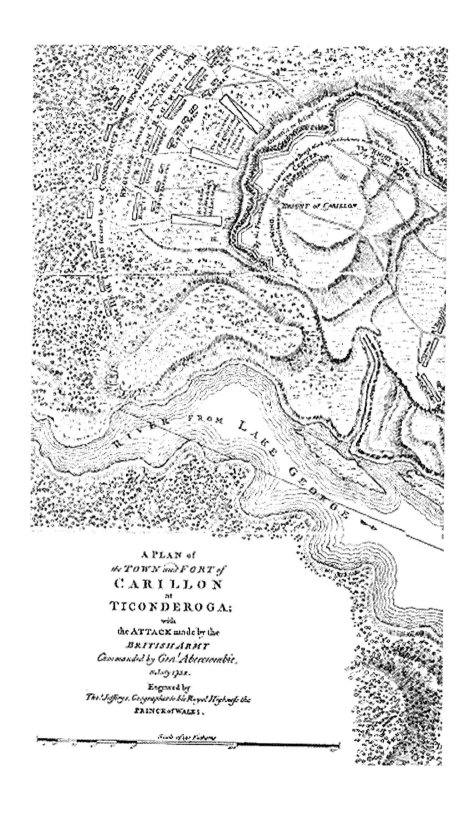

A PLAN of
the TOWN and FORT of
CARILLON
at
TICONDEROGA;
with
the ATTACK made by the
BRITISH ARMY
Commanded by Genl. Abercrombie,
8 July 1758.

Engraved by
Tho. Jefferys, Geographer to his Royal Highness the
PRINCE of WALES.

Scale of 60 Fathoms

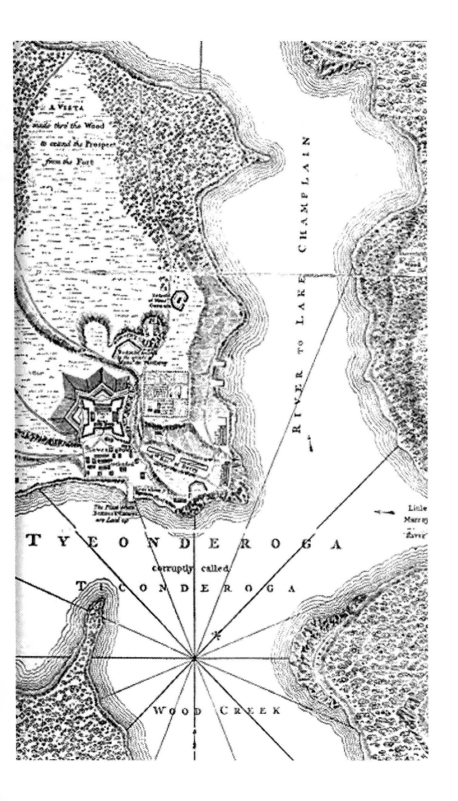

being likewise sensible of my own unfitness for a military life I have resolved to quit the Army as soon as I can obtain leave to resign my commission. But as I have nothing else in the world to depend upon and finding myself at present at a distance from my family and friends or anyone whom I can depend on for advice, interest or assistance and having frequently experienced your goodness and favour, I have made bold to apply to you that you would be pleased to intercede with his Excellency the Earl of Loudon, in my behalf that His Lordship in consideration of my distressed situation and circumstances might be moved to give me leave to resign in favour of some person that would be willing to allow me wherewithal to support me till I can settle and apply to some other way of life.

In doing me this favour you'll forever oblige, Sir, Your respectful and gratefully obed't hum. serv't, *George Maclagan*, Ens.

P. S. If it is agreeable to your Lordship I am willing to pay fifty pound Sterling for Mr. Peter Grant Volunteer.

With these two dispatches from the British War Office as a clue I have tried to learn more about the winter quarters of the Black Watch and have looked through the Colonial manuscript in the New York State Library,[1] the

---

1. The only reference to the Black Watch that I could find in the unpublished Colonial Manuscripts in the N.Y. State Library was the report of the receipt at New York, 8th July, 1757, from the ship *Free Mason* of 22 Bales, 10 Casks and 1 Box for Lord John Murray's Regiment. Colonial Mss., 1757, Vol. 84, Page 126.

Records of the City of Albany and the published works of the period but so far without success. I have been unable to find any Schenectady records of this period. It seems that a valuable collection of Glen-Sanders papers from the old Mansion across the Mohawk from Schenectady was recently sold and I have been told that in these there were several references to officers of the Black Watch.

As the Glens[1] were Scots it would be quite likely that if this collection were not now scattered to the four winds much information about the Highlanders could be obtained. It is said that Schenectady was only a frontier village in 1756 and not large enough to take care of a regiment and it seems to be a fact from the reference given above that only a part of the thousand men were stationed here as it states that the Regiment was stretched along the Mohawk from Schenectady to the German Flats, but that it was a station for troops is proven by the list in the Public Record Office of the winter quarters for the troops in America for 1758, which states that the Black Watch was quartered in New York and Lt. General Murray's at Schenectady. There is in the Public Record Office no list of winter quarters of the troops in America previous to 1758.

---

1. Col. John Glen, born July 2, 1735, died September 23, 1828, was quartermaster during the French and Indian and also the Revolutionary wars and was a man of great prominence in this locality. His brother, Col. Henry Glen, born July 13, 1739, died January 6, 1814, was deputy quartermaster under his brother and was member of Congress from Albany District from 1794 to 1802. Schenectady at that time was in Albany District. It was Col. John Glen who gave the name to Glens Falls, changing it from Wing's Falls, it is said as the result of a wine supper.

It appears, however, from the Town Records of Stamford, Conn., that a committee representing that town made a claim on the "General Court" of the Colony of Connecticut to reimburse them for £369-13-4½d which the town had expended "in taking care of the Highlanders from November 30, 1757, to March 30, 1758. The soldiers numbered 250 officers and men and they had also belonging to them 17 women and 9 children." They were probably part of the Black Watch. The only other Highland regiments of that time were Montgomery's and Fraser's, both raised in 1757 and their arrival at New York from Halifax is noted in reports of April 11, 1757. This town record also further illustrates the custom of that time as previously stated and as an officer of the present Regiment aptly puts it, "they took not only their mess plate but their wives also, on service with them, and sometimes lost both." This 250 at Stamford would only be a quarter of the Regiment, however, if Loudon had upwards of a thousand at or near Schenectady the winter before and it is probable that the rest were quartered at or near Schenectady as in 1756.

Another statement that I have tried to confirm is the account by James Grant in his *Legends of the Black Watch* of the 50 chosen men under orders of MacGillivray of Glen Arrow, who went to reinforce Col. Munro at Fort William Henry. It is also said in a footnote of Wilson's Orderly Book that Capt. Gordon Graham was at Fort William Henry at the time of the surrender, and this is repeated in N.Y. Colonial Mss. by O'Callaghan, page 728, Vol. 10, but I have not been able to find any other reference that would substantiate these statements.

The only time the 42nd emerges from the haze of mystery from June, 1756, to the spring of 1758, is that they were a part of Loudon's expedition against Louisbourg in 1757, and this was more a summer vacation than an act of war.

If the English could have attacked Louisbourg in the spring or early summer, success would have been certain but Loudon couldn't seem to get started. As a messenger from the Governor of Pennsylvania, who had waited in vain for a reply to a message, said about him he was like "St. George on a tavern sign, always on horseback and never riding on." The expedition did not start[1] from New York until June 20th and entered Halifax harbour the 30th. Even after this delay he was there before Admiral Holbourne, who did not arrive from England with his fleet of 15 ships-of-the-line and 3 frigates, with 5,000 troops until July 10th. Then there was more delay, the 12,000 troops were landed and weeks spent in drilling and planting vegetables for their refreshment. Lord Charles Hay was put under arrest for saying that the "nation's money was spent in sham battles and raising cabbages." The troops were embarked again, but Aug. 4th a sloop came from Newfoundland bringing news of the arrival of three French squadrons at Louisbourg and as an attack after this reinforcement would be hopeless, the costly enterprise was abandoned and Loudon and the troops sailed back to New York where he arrived Aug. 31st. Delay was the ruin of the Louisbourg expedition and drew off British forces from the frontier where they were most needed.

---

1. The troops were started immediately up the Hudson as soon as they were landed at New York but Fort William Henry had already been captured Aug. 9th and the French forces had fallen back to Ticonderoga.

CHAPTER 3

The Ticonderoga Campaign

The spring of 1758 opened up with bright prospects. Lord Loudon had been recalled and General Abercrombie, with the able assistance of Lord Howe, was in command. Admiral Boscowen was appointed to command the fleet and Major-General Amherst and Brigadier-Generals Wolfe, Townsend and Murray were added to the military staff. Three expeditions were proposed for this year, Louisbourg, Ticonderoga and Crown Point, and Fort Du-Quesne. The army in America had been largely reinforced during the winter and spring. Of these reinforcements the 42nd was strengthened by three additional companies and recruits bringing the Regiment up to about 1,300 men.

As we have considerable information about these three companies through the Atholl Records, it will be interesting to turn back and follow them from the start to the beginning of the Ticonderoga campaign. The first item and one of interest because it shows the method of raising companies in those days, is a letter from the Duke of Argyll to the Duke of Atholl, dated London, July 9, 1757:[1]

My Lord
This is to acquaint your Grace that there is to be 3

---

1. Atholl Records, page 428, Vol. III.

additional Companies raised for Lord John Murray's Regiment. I believe the nomination of the officers will be left to me and consequently to Your Grace; there will be 3 captains, 6 lieutenants and 3 ensigns and 100 men each company. The raising the men will be the merit of those who shall desire to be officers and if any can be found who have served in Holland, so much the better. Your Grace will have your thought on this but don't promise anybody till you let me hear from you. I shall speak to Lord John but I will bid him consult you and will plainly tell him that the commissions must all be given gratis. The other two Highland Regiments will likewise have the same addition made to them.

I am with the greatest truth and respect, My Lord, Yr Gr's most faithful and obt. h'ble Servant,

Argyll

By the Duke of Atholl's recommendation the three companies were given to James Stewart of Urrard; James Murray, nephew of the Duke of Atholl and son of Lord George Murray; and Thomas Stirling of Ardoch. Three of the new subalterns were from the Atholl estate, namely Lieut. Alexander Menzies and Ensigns Duncan Stewart, son of Derculich, and George Rattray, son of. Dalralzion. The three companies were mustered in October and marched from Perth to Glasgow, where they remained until November 15, when they marched to Greenock and embarked December 1st in transports for Cork en route to America.

April 22, 1758, Capt. James Murray wrote from New York to Mr. Murray of Strowan announcing his safe arrival after a voyage of eleven weeks from Cork. The joys of a voyage in those times when it could take ten days to sail from Scotland to Ireland, is illustrated by a letter from Capt. Murray, dated Youghall, 11 Dec., 1757:

My Dear Brother

This is to let you know that I am just now in good health and safely arrived here with my company. My transport, together with the other five, set sail on the 1st cur't in the evening along with the Convoy; we had a fair wind and good weather until Sunday, early in the morning (when we were past Waterford in our way to Cork) about eight, there came on one of the most prodigious storms that the sailors said they had never seen the like before. About two in the afternoon we lost sight of the Convoy and all the transports and have not yet any sure accounts whether they have got all safe into harbours or not. But since I came here I hear that there was five or six ships lost on the Coast that day. The storm abated somewhat Monday morning but it continued bad weather until Friday evening, during which time we were often in risk of our lives especially twice, once being within two yards of a great rock and the other time when we were on two fathom water going on a sandbank.

During all that time we were near several harbours, such as Dublin, Waterford, Cork and others but all without success. Saturday and this day we had good weather by which means we got into harbour.

Your most aff'te brother,

James Murray

From November until April seems a long voyage from Scotland to America even in those days of primitive navigation, but another of the three additional companies was blown into Antigua and did not arrive at New York until June.

With the activities of the preparations for the Ticonderoga campaign a number of dispatches were sent to the Home Government and it is possible to follow more closely the fortunes of the Black Watch.

The addition of these three companies raised the Regiment to 1,300 men, and we find among the official documents a petition from Capt. Gordon Graham, endorsed by Lt. Col. Grant and General Abercrombie, asking to be made Major in addition to Major Duncan Campbell, as follows:[1]

> To His Excellency James Abercromby. Esq.
>
> General and Commander in Chief of all His Majesty's forces in North America, etc., etc., etc.
>
> The Memorial of Gordon Graham, eldest Captain in His Majesty's 42nd Regiment of Foot in America.
>
> Humbly sheweth
>
> That your memorialist hath had the honour to serve His Majesty upwards of twenty-five years, twelve of which as Captain in the above Regiment and is now eldest in that Rank.
>
> That he hath served in Flanders and elsewhere during all the last war, some part of which he was employed as Major of Brigade, and had a commission as such from General St. Clair, on the expedition under his command in the year 1746.

---

1. Public Record Office W. O. 1.-1.

May it therefore please your Excellency to lay his case before His Majesty that he in his great wisdom may be graciously pleased to promote him to the Rank of Major when an opportunity offers, all which is humbly submitted.

To His Excellency, James Abercromby, Esqr.

General and Commander in Chief of all his Majesty's forces in North America, etc., etc., etc.

The Memorial of Colonel Francis Grant, Commanding his Majesty's 42nd Regiment of Foot.

Humbly sheweth

That his Majesty having thought proper to augment the said Regiment to 1,300 men by adding three additional companies to it, and such a body of men being too numerous to be exercised and disciplined by one Major only, your memoralist humbly conceives, that it would be for the good of his Majesty's service to have another Major added, as has been already done to the other two Highland Battalions commanded by the Colonels Montgomery and Fraser.

May it therefore please your Excellency to Vay this matter before His Majesty that he in his great wisdom may be graciously pleased to give such directions thereupon as shall be thought necessary, all which is humbly submitted.

Col. Grant, commanding His Majesty's 42nd Regiment, and Mr. Gordon Graham, a Captain in the same, having each of them presented me with a memorial, the contents of which I know to be true, I herewith transmit them to your Lordship, to be laid before the King, and to know His Royal Pleasure therein.[1]

As will be seen later Capt. Graham became Major before hearing from the King. The next dispatch which is of interest and which makes changes in the list of Commissioned Officers is as follows:

In the list of the Commissions which I had the honour to transmit to your Lordship, by my last letter, you will have observed two vacancies in the 42nd Regiment, occasioned by the removal of Sir James Cockburn into the 48th which could not be filled up at the time my letter went away, as the gentlemen, whom it was proposed should purchase those vacancies were then at Albany, and their answer not arrived; since that the Lieutenancy has been made out in the name of Mr. Patrick Balnevas, and bears date the 1st of April; and Mr. Elbert Hering succeeds to the Ensigncy, dated the 3rd of the same month.[2]

Then we have the dispatch just before the battle from Abercrombie to Pitt, dated Camp at Lake George, June 29, 1758, saying:

Arrived Fort Edward on the 9th, where Lord Howe was encamped with the 42nd, 44th, and 55th Regiments and 4 companies of Rangers. Remainder of Regulars were at posts below on Hudson River

1. Extract from a letter signed James Abercromby to the Right Hon. Lord Viscount Barrington, dated New York, Apr. 28, 1758.
2. Extract from letter signed by James Abercromby to the Right Honorable the Lord Viscount Barrington, dated Albany, May 27, 1758. Public record office.

and were working up the stores, etc. On the 17th Lord Howe marched to the Brook, half way between Fort Edward and the Lake with the 42nd, 44th, and 55th. This Half-way Brook was judged a proper post for the first Deposit in a Portage of 15 miles. 3 After the carriages had made several trips Lord Howe advanced to the Lake with the 42nd, 44th, and 55th.[1]

Attached to this letter is a report of troops at Lake George, June 29, 1758, and the roll of the 42nd was:

10 companies
1 Lt. Colonel
1 Major
8 Captains
18 Lieutenants
7 Ensigns
1 Chaplain
1 Adjutant
1 Quarter Master
1 Surgeon
2 Mates
40 Sergeants
18 Drummers
Rank and File 981 fit for duty
11 sick present
6 in general hospital
2 on command
1,000 total
1 drummer and 40 rank and file to complete.

---

1. His last letter had been written from New York April 8th. If this were an earlier date it might indicate the winter quarters but at this time the army was assembling at Albany for the seasons campaign. It will be noted as illustration that the Highlanders quartered at Stamford.

We find the solution of why there were only 1,000 of the Black Watch with the Ticonderoga expedition when its strength was known to be 1,300 at that time, in another extract of the Report of June 29th from Abercrombie to Pitt:

> I have left two additional Companies of Lord John Murray's to garrison Fort Edward. The other additional company of the 42nd which was blown into Antego (Antigua), I hear is arrived at New York, which I have ordered up to Albany.

This is confirmed in more detail in a letter from Sir Robert Menzies to Mr. Murray of Strowan, dated Rannock, 6th September, 1758, in which is an extract from a letter received by Menzies from "Jamie Stewart."[1]

> That, after the additional Companies arrived in Fort Edward, the best men were picked out to complete the Regiment in place of the sick and old men that were put in their place. That, as Capt. Reid was left behind sick at Albany, Capt. Murray was appointed to his company and Reid to the additionals, as Capt. Abercrombie was to Capt. Murray's Company. That the additional companies, with Captains Sterling, Reid, and Abercrombie, etc., were left at Fort Edward, where they had nothing to do but to garrison the Fort and divert themselves.

Everything is now in readiness for the attack on Ticonderoga and an army of six thousand three hundred seventy-seven regulars and nine thousand thirty-four provincials (Abercrombie to Pitt July 12, 1758) embarked at Lake George early on the morning of July 5th. There were nine

---

1. Atholl Records page, 444 Vo. III.

hundred *batteaux*, a hundred and thirty-five whale boats and a large number of heavy flat-boats carrying the artillery and from front to rear the line was six miles long.

Parkman in his *Montcalm and Wolfe* paints the scene as follows:

The spectacle was superb; the brightness of the summer day; the romantic beauty of the scenery; the sheen and sparkle of those crystal waters; the countless islets, tufted with pine, birch, and fir; the bordering mountains, with their green summits and sunny crags; the flash of oars and glitter of weapons; the banners, the varied uniforms, and the notes of bugle, trumpet, bag-pipe, and drum, answered and prolonged by a hundred woodland echoes. 'I never beheld so delightful a prospect' wrote a wounded officer at Albany a fortnight after.

Rogers with the Rangers, and Gage with the light infantry, led the way in whaleboats, followed by Bradstreet with his corps of boatman, armed and drilled as soldiers. Then came the main body. The central column of regulars was commanded by Lord Howe, his own regiment, the fifty-fifth, in the van, followed by the Royal Americans, the twenty-seventh, forty-fourth, forty-sixth, and eightieth infantry, and the Highlanders of the forty-second, with their major, Duncan Campbell of Inverawe, silent and gloomy amid the general cheer, for his soul was dark with foreshadowings of death. With this central column came what are described as two floating castles, which were no doubt batteries to cover the landing of the troops. On the right hand and the left

ABERCROMBIES ARMY EMBARKING AT LAKE GEORGE, JULY 5TH 1758

were the provincials, uniformed in blue, regiment after regiment, from Massachusetts, Connecticut, New
York, New Jersey, and Rhode Island. Behind them
all came the *batteaux*, loaded with stores and baggage, and the heavy flatboats that carried the artillery,
while a rear-guard of provincials and regulars closed
the long procession.

It will be unnecessary to go into the details of this dis-
astrous campaign, but briefly, the army landed at the foot
of Lake George the morning of the 6th and the afternoon of the same day Lord Howe at the head of a Ticonderoga party was killed at the outlet of Trout Brook. This
is the beginning of the end as Lord Howe was the real
head of the army. Abercrombie took until the eighth to
make up his mind what to do and this interim gave the
French time to build the fatal breastworks across the
ridge about one-half mile west of the Fort and enabled
Levis to arrive with reinforcements. As the breastworks
play a most important part in the Battle it will perhaps
be well to again quote from Parkman who gives a most
comprehensive description.

> The trees that covered the ground were hewn
> down by thousands, the tops lopped off, and the
> trunks piled one upon another to form a massive
> breastwork. The line followed the top of the ridge,
> along which it zigzagged in such a manner that the
> whole front could be swept by flank-fires of mus-
> ketry and grape. It was so high that nothing could
> be seen over it but the crowns of the soldiers' hats.
> The upper tier was formed of single logs, in which
> notches were cut to serve as loopholes; and in some

places sods and bags of sand were piled along the top, with narrow spaces to fire through. From the central part of the line the ground sloped away like a natural glacis; while at the sides, and especially on the left, it was undulating and broken. Over this whole space, to the distance of a musket shot from the works, the forest was cut down, and the trees left lying where they fell among the stumps, with tops turned outwards, forming one vast abattis, which, as a Massachusetts officer says, looked like a forest laid flat by a hurricane. But the most formidable obstruction was immediately along the front of the breastworks, where the ground was covered with heavy boughs, overlapping and interlaced, with sharpened points bristling into the face of the assailant like the quills of a porcupine. As these works were all of wood, no vestige of them remains. The earthworks now shown to tourists as the lines of Montcalm were begun four days after the battle to replace the log breastwork; and though on the same ground are not on the same plan.

Behind these breastworks the battalions of LaSarre and Languedoc were posted on the left under Bourlamaque, the first battalion of Berry with that of Royal Roussillon in the center under Montcalm and those of LaReine, Beam and Guienne on the right under Levis. A detachment of volunteers occupied the low grounds between the breastworks and the outlet of Lake George and on the side toward Lake Champlain were stationed 450 regulars and Canadians, about 3,600 in all.

It is always easy to criticise an event after it has occurred, but the result certainly shows that Abercrombie could not have planned his campaign more to the advantage of the French. He first gave them time to build those formidable breastworks and then instead of choosing any one of half a dozen plans which would have brought victory, he decided to throw his army unsupported by artillery, which was still at Lake George, at the strongest part of the French position, he himself staying in safety at the sawmill a mile and a half in the rear of his army.[1]

The sad result is too well known to dwell on and we pass at once to the part played by the Black Wateh. They, with the 55th were to have formed the reserve but impatient at being left in the rear the Highlanders could not be restrained and were soon in the front endeavouring to cut their way through the fallen trees with their broadswords. Captain John Campbell, who was one of the two soldiers presented to George II in 1743, with a few men, were the only ones to force their way over the breastworks and they were instantly dispatched with the bayonet.

Lieut. William Grant of the Regiment writes as follows:

> The attack began a little past one in the afternoon and about two the fire became general on both sides. It was exceedingly heavy and without intercession insomuch as the oldest soldier never saw so furious and incessant a fire. The fire at Fontenoy was nothing to it. I saw both.

An officer of the 55th regiment, of which Lord Howe had been the commander, wrote as follows:

---

1. This General James Abercrombie must not be confused with Sir Ralph Abercrombie who led the Black Watch to victory in Egypt.
2. Translation by Bell, Page 539, Vol. I.

> With a mixture of esteem, grief and envy, I am penetrated by the great loss and immortal glory acquired by the Highlanders engaged in the late bloody affair. Impatient for the fray, they rushed forward to the entrenchments which many of them actually mounted, their intrepidity was rather animated than dampened by witnessing their comrades fall on every side. They seemed more anxious to avenge the fate of their deceased friends than to avoid a like death. In their co-operation we trust soon to give a good account of the enemy and of ourselves. There is much harmony and friendship between the two regiments.

Even the French were impressed with the valour of the Black Watch as Garneau writes in *L'Histoire du Canada*.[2]

> The Highlanders above all, under Lord John Murray, covered themselves with glory. They formed the head of the troops confronting the Canadians, their light and picturesque costume distinguishing them from all other soldiers amid the flame and smoke. This corps lost half of its men and 25 of its officers were killed or severely wounded.

Lossing writes, "The whole army seemed envious to excel but the Scotch Highland Regiment of Lord John Murray was foremost in the conflict and suffered the severest loss."[1]

The following letters from Captain Allan Campbell are of interest:

---

1. Lossing's *Pictorial Field Book of the Revolution*. Page 119. Vol. 1.

Camp at Lake George
11th July, 1758
Dr. Broyr

The 8th of this month we had a hot brush at the lines of Ticonderoga where we lost a considerable number of men and officers. The officers of your acquaintance wounded are Major Campbell and his son. Both in their arms, and I hope will do well. Captain Stratchur slightly in the breast, Ltt. Archd. Campbell Sheriff badly in the Breast, Lt. John Campbell Glendaruel slightly in the arm, Capt. Ltt. John Campbell Duneaves killed, Ltt. Hugh Macpherson ditto, Capt. Graham, Duchra, and Broyr. Both wounded slightly and several other offrs. of the Regt. but not of your acquaintance are killed and wounded.

Our Regt. acquired great glory by their good behaviour of both men and officers, tho' we were unsuccessful!. I have the pleasure to acquaint you that both my nephew George and I escaped without a scratch, tho' both in the heat of the action. George is a pretty Lad: he's now a Ltt. in Coll. Gages Regt. of Lt. Infantry. Your son the Major was well about 2 months ago at Philadelphia. We are now at the end of Lake George encamped. I have told you now all the news that can occur to me or that I have time to write you, and I thought it my duty to acquaint you and my other Broyrs. of my being well after a smart action. I have no time to write you more being excessively hurried having no body to assist me in the affairs of my Company having my three Ltts. killed or wounded *viz.* Ltt. Balie killed and Ltts.

Archd. Campbell and William Grant wounded. I'll write you very fully in my next. My best wishes to my sister, to your family and all our friends, and I am Dr. Broyr, your most affec. and Lov. Broyr, while
Allan Campbell

New York
6th January 1759
Dr. Brother

I wrote you the 11th July in a great hurry after our retreat from Ticonderoga to let you know of mine and George's welfare, after that unlucky affair, where several of our friends and a great many worthy Fellows suffer'd. Our Regt. lost more than any other Corps at the attack of the Lines. We have had killed and wounded since the beginning of the Campaign 520 (officers included) of which about 300 were left dead on the field or have died of their wounds, and of 37 officers that were present with the Regt. that day 11 only came off unhurt, of which number I was lucky enough to be one.

You would certainly hear before now of poor Major Campbell Inveraw's death, he liv'd about a fortnight after he receiv'd his wound, the Doctors thought it necessary that his arm should be cut off, and he died soon after the operation at Fort Edward, all the rest of our wounded officers are quite recover'd except his son, Sandy, Jock Campbell Glendaruel, and Archie Shirreff, but they are out of all danger, only their cure will be tedious.

Poor George had a narrow escape the day we landed at the French end of the Lake, having had a scratch along the face with a musket ball. He was in a smart little action that happen'd in the woods a month afterwards between a detachment of 500 of our army under the command of Major Rogers and much the same number of Indians French and Canadians, where the latter were repulsed with the loss of 100 men, and I assure you his behaviour at that affair was much applauded by his Broyr. officers on their return to the Army.

He's now second oldest Lieut. in General Gage's Regt. of light arm'd infantry, for which he's obliged to the late Major Campbell Inveraw; and as they talk at present of augmenting that corps, he'll have a good chance of getting higher up, and in any event he's better off by being so high in that Regt. as they are now an establish'd Corps, than if he had stayed in ours, where he could be but a young Lieut. His Col. has a great regard for him, and very deservedly for he's a lad of good morals, a good spirit, and very fit for his business. He has acted as Adjutant to that Regt. since July last, by which he has nothing yet but treble, there being no Adjutant allow'd, and that his Colonel means it for him; if he's lucky enough to get that, I think he's very well provided for for the time he has served.

I have advanc'd him Twenty Guineas for which he gave me a bill on you. I hope you'll not disapprove of my conduct for doing it, nor blame him for running so much short, when I explain to you the cause of it; its true he came over very well rigged out, but his changing Corps put him under a necessity of

buying new Regimentals, as these differ in Colours
from the rest of the Army, being Brown, besides his
expense must be greater upon his first coming in
among Strangers, and he had the misfortune of being sent a recruiting last winter, which really is a
misfortune to an officer in this Country unless he is
very careful and happens to be successful, and I believe George lost by it. This I assure you is truth, and
when you consider it was owing to these accidents,
that he could not possibly guard against, I am hope-
ful you'll easily forgive him. I was likewise oblig'd
to advance our tinkle Corries' son, Colin, Twenty
two Pounds eighteen shillings and tenpence or he
must have gone naked, having lost all his things at
Fort William Henry. I have sent both Bills to Brother
Robert. George and Colin are sent this winter a recruiting to Pennsylvania.

I had a letter dated the 30 Novr. from my nephew, the Major, from where Fort du Quesne stood,
he was then very well. I expect daily to hear from
him, he's had as troublesome and fatiguing Campaign of it, as ever any body had, our Army has
been above a month in Winter Quarters before
theirs got to Fort du Quesne, which the French
burnt upon their near approach, and an immense
long march they have to get back to Philadelphia,
where their Regt. is to be quarter'd this winter, and
where I intend to go and see him, when I hear of
their arrival, its about 100 miles from this place that
our Regt. is now quarter'd in.

We long much for a packet here having been no

news from Europe for some months, I take the opportunity of writing you now by the *Kennington* Man of War that carries home General Abercrombie. . . .

There is no news here at present. All our friends in this country are well. Remember my best wishes to my sister, and the rest of your family whom may God Almighty bless and I ever am, Dr. Brother, your affec. and Lov. Broyr.[1]

Allan Campbell

I also give in full the letter written by Capt. James Murray to his brother, Mr. Murray of Strowan, dated Albany, July 19, 1758, as his description of the country and the events during and after the battle lend colour to the picture.[2]

My Dear Brother

The last letter I wrote you was dated from Fort Edward camp about 18th June. We proceeded on to Lake George where Fort William Henry formerly

---

1. Some of the names in the two preceding letters from Capt. Campbell are interesting because they illustrate the Scottish custom of using name of estate rather than the family or given name. This was often necessary to distinguish between several of same name. Captain Stratchur is Captain John Campbell of Stratchur, there are also John Campbells of Duneavis, and of Glendaruel. Archie Sherreff is Lieut. Archibald Campbell, son of the Sheriff of Argyle. Duchra is Capt. Thomas Graeme of Duchray. George and "the Major" are sons of John Campbell of Barcaldine George Campbell was appointed Ensign in the 42nd in 1756, promoted Lieut. in Gage's Regiment 1757, and killed at Havana 1762. "The Major" was Alexander Campbell, Major in the 77th (Montgomery Highlanders). Unkle Corries is John Campbell of Corries and his son Colin was evidently at the massacre at Fort William Henry in August 1757. Fort du Quesne was the French fort at what is now Pittsburgh.

2. Atholl Records. Page 438, Vol. 3.

stood which was taken and destroyed by the French last year, where we remained until the 5th curt, and then the whole army embarked on the lake in *batteaux* that hold 23 men with a month's provisions all the artillery stores was likewise embarked, and everything else belonging to an army. We were divided into brigades. There was in all about 5,000 regulars and 12,000 provincials. We had also light infantry and rangers who had whale-boats which are the lightest and best going boats that can be made. We put off about 8 and got fairly into the lake which I took to be about 20 miles long and not above two miles at the broadest part of it. There are several small islands which are quite covered with wood and all around the lake is very hilly and quite covered with woods, as the most part of the country is, at least what I have seen of it.

This lake abounds in fine trout the meat of which is red, perch, suckers and several other sorts of fish. There is also plenty of beavers. On the side of the lake there is plenty of deer but I have not seen any since I came to the country. Sometimes when I have been out on command I have killed rattle snakes about four feet long and as thick as the small of one's leg, with 18 rattles, which altogether might be about four inches long. They say some have twenty or more. They have both teeth and a sting. The rattles being at the tail makes them that they can stand up on end and spring a short way at one. When touched they make a great noise with their rattles. Their bite is not so bad as called for it can be easily cured with oil or

The Black Watch at Ticonderoga, July 8th 1758

salt. They smell exactly like a goat, rather ranker if possible before they are seized but afterwards have almost no smell at all. They make the richest and best soup that can be which I eat of and like much. The meat is but insipid.

The 6th we disembarked at the lower end of the lake. In the morning out light infantry and rangers had some skirmishing with the French pickets. Lord Howe was killed at the second shot and he is very much regretted. There was taken that day about 150 prisoners, five of whom were officers. They had a great many killed so that very few of their pickets escaped which consisted in all of about 350.

The next day being the 7th, we were making preparations to invest a fort called Theenderora which is five miles from Lake George and is situate on a neck of land that runs into Lake Champlain. As to the dimensions of that lake I can't say, and marched within a mile and half of it that evening. The next morning the light infantry made the French sentries and small posts retire to their entrenchments for the French had an encampment about half a cannon shot before their fort, and were entrenched after the following manner: They had large cut trees one laid above another a man's height and in the outside there was brush and logs for about 15 paces from it which made it impossible to force their breastworks without cannon which we had not taken up that length as then. They were also under cover of the fort or if we could beat them out of their trenches, they could have retired pretty safely.

Between one and two we marched up and attacked the trenches and got within twenty paces of them and had as hot a fire for about three hours as possibly could be, we all the time seeing but their hats and the end of their muskets. About half an hour before we were obliged to retire I received a shot through my thigh after which I stayed a few minutes but finding if I stayed any longer my thigh would turn stiff and losing a great deal of blood I with help got into the road and that evening with Capt. Gordon Graham, our paymaster, got into a whaleboat and against the next morning got to the upper end of Lake George and was transported down here. I am confined to my bed but the surgeons say my wound looks as well as can be expected, nor is there any sort of danger in it as it has only grazed the bone, so I shall be well soon again. I am in perfect good health, have a good appetite and sleep tolerably well.

Our regiment has suffered much. There was the captain, lieutenant and six subalterns killed on the spot and since the major and the lieutenant have died of their wounds. The colonel, four captains, and twelve subalterns are wounded. 180 men killed and 280 wounded. None of the other regiments' losses were near so great. Capt. Stewart was not touched, Capt. Sterling nor Farquharson were not there so are well, but Lieut. Farquharson's younger brother was killed. Lieut. David Mills, my lieutenant, is not ill wounded and is pretty well, so if you would inform his father-inlaw, Mr. Hamilton, of Hutcheson, who stays near Glasgow, you would oblige me. Neil Stewart at Perth knows him.

I received a letter from Lord John 15th May letting me know you are all well which gave me a great deal of pleasure but it would much more so to hear from some of you for it is very long since I had that satisfaction, the last being at Ireland, for Lord John wrote me no particulars.

Offer my humble duty to my dear mother and elsewhere due and best love to dear Lady Charlotte, Lady Sinclair, George, Charlotte and Invercauld, and my best blessing attend all the young ones. My kind compliments to Shusy Moray and tell her I had her hair about my neck when I received my wound which might have probably gone to my heart if it had not been wounded already. I am ever your most affectionate brother,

James Murray

Thus had the army which landed so proudly two days before been disastrously repulsed, with a loss in killed and wounded and missing of nineteen hundred and forty-four officers and men. In his report of July 12, 1758, Abercrombie gives the casualty of the 42nd as follows:

KILLED

Capt. Lt. John Campbell
Lieutenants George Farquharson, Hugh McPherson, William Bailey, (John Sutherland; Ensigns Peter Stewart and George Rattray.

WOUNDED

Major Duncan Campbell
Captains Gordon Graham, Thomas Graeme, John Campbell, James Stewart, James Murray
Lieutenants William Grant, Robert Gray, John Campbell, James Grant, John Graham, Alexander Campbell, Alexander McIntosh, Archibald Campbell, David Mill,[1] Patrick Balnevis
Ensigns John Smith and Peter Grant.

SUMMARY

1 major wounded, captains 1 killed, 4 wounded; lieutenants 4 killed, 11 wounded; ensigns 2 killed, 2 wounded; adjutants 1 wounded; quarter master 1 wounded; sergeants 6 killed, 13 wounded, rank and file 190 killed, 265 wounded.

Stewart of Garth writes as follows:

Of these the 42nd regiment had 8 officers, 9 Sergeants, and 297 men killed, and 17 officers, 10 Sergeants, and 306 soldiers wounded. The officers were:

KILLED

Major Duncan Campbell of Inverawe
Captain John Campbell
Lieutenants George Farquharson, Hugh McPherson, William Baillie and John Sutherland
Ensigns Patrick Stewart of Bonskied and George Rattray

---

1. This name is given in various places as Miles, Mills, Milder and Milne. The Duke of Atholl is authority for the statement.

WOUNDED

Captains Gordon Graham, Thomas Graham of Duchray, John Campbell of Strachur, James Stewart of Urrad, James Murray (afterward General)
Lieutenants James Grant, Robert Gray, John Campbell, William Grant, John Graham, Alexander Campbell, Alexander Mackintosh, Archibald Campbell, David Miller, Patrick Balneaves
Ensigns John Smith and Peter Grant

Capt. James Murray writes from Albany 17th August, 1758:[1]

As I observed in my last, our regiment has suffered greatly. The Major has since died of his wounds, Sandy Farquharson has got his lieutenancy by seniority which one would not have thought that the youngest ensign of the additionals would have been so soon a lieutenant. I am recovering pretty well and can walk about although I am much pained in my knee but hope will be able to soon joint the regiment.

Capt. James Stewart writes 14th July from Lake George that:[2]

.... all the Captains were wounded, less or more, excepting Captains McNeil and Allan Campbell, that Major Campbell got his right arm wounded, but not dangerous and his son, Lieutenant Alexander Campbell had his arm broke betwixt the elbow and shoulder, but he was in a good way.

---

1. Atholl Records, p. 444, Vol. III.
2. Atholl Records, p. 443, Vol. III.

Parkman states that Lt. Alexander Campbell was severely wounded but reached Scotland alive and died in Glasgow.[1] Abercrombie reports to Pitt from Lake George, Aug. 19, 1758:

> Major Duncan Campbell of the 42nd who was wounded in the arm at the battle on the 8th was obliged to have it cut off and died soon thereafter.[2]

It would seem therefore that the wounds of Major Campbell and his son were not necessarily fatal and that modern surgery would have cured them. The following however, taken from Garneau's *L'Histoire du Canada* might explain the unexpected mortality.

> Scarcely any of the wounded Highlanders ever recovered and even those sent home as invalids; their sores cankered, owing to the broken glass, ragged bits of metal, etc., used by the Canadians instead of shot.[3]

Or this extract from letter of Brig. General James Wolfe to Lord George Sackville:

Halifax
24th May 1758

> Some of the Regiments of this Army have 300 or 400 men eat up with the scurvy. All of them that are wounded or hurt by any accident run great risks of their lives from the corrupted state of the blood.

> The curious part of the barbarity is that the scoundrels of Contractors can afford the fresh meat in many places and circumstances as cheap as the salt.

---

1. Montcalm and Wolfe, p. 435, Vol. II.
2. Public Record Office, C.O.5. 50.
3. Translation by Bell, page 539, Vol. I.

Abercrombie states in his report of July 12, 1758:

> I sent the wounded officers and the men that could be moved to Fort Edward and Albany.

Major Campbell was sent to Fort Edward and upon his death nine days after the battle he was buried in the family lot of the Gilchrists, in the old cemetery at Fort Edward. The body was moved to the Gilchrist lot in the new Union cemetery between Sandy Hill and Fort Edward in 1871, and in 1920 was moved again to the Jane McCrea lot in the same cemetery. The original stone may still be seen and bears the inscription:

Here Lyes the body of
Duncan Campbell of Inversaw, Esqr
Major to the old Highland Regt.

Aged 55 Years.

Who died the 17th July, 1758, of wounds he received in the attack of the retrenchments of Ticonderoga or Carillon, 8th July, 1758.

Stewart of Garth says:

> The old Highland Regiment having suffered so severely. . . . they were not employed again that year.

In the N. Y. Colonial Records, however, we find that some regulars of the 42nd and 6th Regts. amounting to 155 men (probably one company of each) were with Bradstreet in his exposition against Fort Frontenac.[1]

In Abercrombie's report of Aug. 19, 1758, he states that part of the additional companies of the 42nd were sent to

---

1. N.Y. Col. manuscript O'Callaghan's, p. 827, Vol. 10.

reinforce Brig. General Provost at Fort Edward and that one company of the 42nd and some of the recovering men were stationed at Albany. From this it might be inferred that the only part of the Black Watch fit for duty were the three additional companies which had not been in the battle of July 8th and it is possible that the one company of the 42nd that had been blown out of its course to Antigua and had not arrived at New York until June did not get further north than Albany. The winter quarters of the 42nd for 1758 were at New York.[1]

The official title is now changed to the "42nd or Royal Regiment of foot," and the regiment is commonly called the Royal Highlanders. It has erroneously been stated that the Black Watch was granted this honour of being a "Royal" regiment because of its gallantry at Ticonderoga, but it is all the more to its credit that it had earned this distinction before the battle at Ticonderoga. The title was granted by special warrant dated July 22, 1758, while the news of the defeat did not reach London until the arrival of Abercrombie's aid-de-camp with dispatches Aug. 20, 1758.

A copy of the warrant is as follows:

George R.

We being desirous to distinguish Our Forty Second Regiment of Foot with some mark of Our Royal favour, Our Will and Pleasure therefore is, and we do hereby direct, that from henceforth

Our said regiment be called, and distinguished by the title and name of Our Forty-Second, or Royal Highland Regiment of Foot, in all commissions, orders, and writings, that shall hereafter be made out,

---

1. Abercrombie to Pitt, No. 25, 1758. Public Record Office C. O. 5: 50.

or issued for and concerning the said regiment. Given at Our Court at Kensington this 22nd day of July 1758, in the thirty second year of Our reign. By His Majesty's command.

(Signed) *Barrington*

The vacancies occasioned in the 42nd were filled up in regular succession and the seven companies which had been ordered at the same time as the change of title were immediately recruited. These were completed in three months and embodied at Perth, October 1758, each company being 120 men strong, all, with few exceptions, Highlanders and hardy and temperate in their habits. (Lord John Murray's orders were preemptory that none but Highlanders be taken, but a few O'Donnels, O'Lachlans and O'Briens passed muster as MacDonnels, MacLachlans and MacBriars.)

These seven companies with the three additional companies raised in 1757 were formed into a Second Battalion. The officers appointed to the seven new companies were Robert Anstruther, who was senior captain and served as Major, Francis MacLean, Alexander Sinclair, John Stewart of Stenton, William Murray of Lintrose, Archibald Campbell, Alexander Reid, and Robert Arbuthnot, to be captains; Alexander MacLean, George Grant, George Sinclair, Gordon Clunes, Adam Stewart, John Robertson, son of Lude, John Grant, James Fraser, George Leslie, John Campbell, Alexander Stewart, Duncan Richardson and Robert Robertson, to be lieutenants and Patrick Sinclair, John Macintosh, James MacDuff, Thomas Fletcher, Alexander Donaldson, William MacLean, and William Brown, to be ensigns.

The seven new companies embarked for the West Indies where they joined with the Old Bluffs, Kings, 6th, 63rd, 64th, 800 marines and a detachment of artillery amounting in all to 5,560 men under the command of Major Generals Hopson and Barrington and of Brigadier Generals Haldane, Armiger, Trapaud and Clavering, in an exposition against Martinique and Gaudaloupe. This resulted in the capture of Gaudaloupe but was not altogether a success and a great many men were lost by fever and sickness. Of the Royal Highlanders Ensign MacLean was killed, Lieutenants MacLean, Leslie, Sinclair and Robertson were wounded, and Major Anstruther and Captain Arbuthnot died of the fever. One hundred and six privates were killed, wounded or died of disease.

This was a severe initiation for the new recruits who had been herding sheep on their native hills nine months before, but as has always been the case with the Black Watch they acquitted themselves with distinction.

The seven companies were then embarked for New York to join the First Battalion where they arrived in July. They just missed being at the capture of Ticonderoga. Major Gordon Graham was ordered at the end of July by General Amherst then at Crown Point to take command of the seven companies and to march them up to Oswego. In August they were ordered to join the First Battalion, Capt. Stewart with 150 men being left at Oswego and the First and Second Battalions, now united, served together for the rest of the campaign.

CHAPTER 4

Beyond the Battle

We will now return to the Veterans of the previous year. After wintering in New York (or on Long Island, as another authority states) the old Black Watch now the first Battalion of the Royal Highlanders, recruited again to its full strength and the three additional companies now a part of the Second Battalion, joined Amherst at Fort Edward in June, 1759.[1] Col. Grant of the 42nd with the Royal Highlanders and light infantry of the army moved forward to Lake George the 20th and the main part of the army followed on the 21st. For five years now Lake George had been the annual mustering place of armies.

The campaign this season comprehended three very important enterprises Wolfe was to attack Quebec from Lower Canada, Prideaux was to proceed against Niagara, and Amherst, now Commander in Chief and successor of General Abercrombie, was to drive the French from Lake Champlain and if possible join Wolfe on the St. Lawrence.

The army under Amherst consisted of the Royals, 17th, 27th, Royal Highlanders, two battalions of the 55th, Montgomery's Highlanders, nine battalions of Provincials, and a battalion of light infantry and a body of Rangers and Indians with a detachment of artillery. When joined by the 2d battalion of the Royal Americans from the West Indies, this army amounted to 14,500 men.

Major Alexander Campbell of the 77th writes from Fort Edward, June 19th, 1759:

> Our General is beloved by his soldiers, honoured and esteem'd by his officers, careful of mens' lives and healths, in short he is the man I would choose to serve under of any I know in the service. Our Regiment are healthy and in high spirits as are the whole army, and I hope we soon will strike a stroke that will bring credit and glory to our General and army and satisfaction to our country and friends.

Amherst never remained long in one place without building a fort. Fortified places were built at intervals of three or four miles along the road to Fort Edward and especially at the station called Halfway Brook, while for the whole distance a broad belt of wood on both sides was cut down and burned to deprive a skulking enemy of cover. At Lake George he started a fort, now called Fort George, the ruins of which are in the Lake George Battle Ground Park of which this Association is custodian.

July 21st, 1759, Lake George again witnessed a military pageant as the army embarked for its second attack on Fort Ticonderoga. At daylight they landed, beat back a French detachment and marched by the portage road to the sawmill. There was little resistance and the army marched to the former line of entrenchments which had proved so fatal to Abercrombie. These had been reconstructed partly of earth and partly of logs, and as the French made no attempt at their defence the English encamped along their front and found them excellent shelter from the cannon of the fort. It is the general impression that the French re-treated with only faint resistance and that there was hardly a shot fired at the second attempt to capture Fort Car-rillon but the following letter from Capt. Murray would correct this impression:

Camp at the Lines of Burning Theanderoga
27 July, 1758
My Dear Brother:
    I write you these few lines to acquaint you that I am in perfect good health and that the army landed at this end of the lake the 22nd, invested the Fort the 23rd and was very busy carrying on the works till the 26th in the night, at which time we had three batteries ready to open, when the enemy abandoned and set fire to the fort. During the time that the en-emy remained they could not keep a hotter fire, for I dare say that fired ten thousand cannon shot and five hundred bombs and I don't believe there has been forty men killed and wounded during that hot fire, altho' all the Bombs fell in different parts among us and that we were nigh point blank of the cannon shot but the line that had been of so much hurt to us last year saved our men this.
    Your most afft. Brother
    James Murray

I also add Amherst's report to Governor James DeLancey:

Camp at Ticonderoga
27th July 1758
Sir:
    On Saturday morning last I embarked with the

army at Lake George, the next day landed without opposition and proceeded to the sawmills, and took post on the commanding grounds, meeting only a trifling opposition from the enemy. We lay on our arms all night and early on the 23rd we continued our march to the ground which I took possession of in the forenoon, the enemy having abandoned the lines without destroying them, first having carried off their effects as well as sent away the greatest part of their troops. As soon as I was set down before the place and after having reconnoitred it, I ordered the trenches to be opened and batteries to be made, which were finished last night, and were to have opened at break of day, but the enemy did not think proper to wait till then, having about ten of the clock yesterday evening blown up a part of the Fort, and made their escape all to about 20 deserters. Our loss considering the fire we sustained is inconsiderable. We have only two officers killed, *viz.* Colonel Townshend, Deputy Adjutant General and Ensign Harrison of late Forbe's.

Bourlamaque had on receipt of orders from Vandreuil retired down Lake Champlain leaving four hundred men under Hebecourt to defend the fort as long as possible and then to abandon Ticonderoga and later when pressed Crown Point and to retreat to Isleoux-Noix at the outlet of Lake Champlain, where defence was to be made to the last extremity.

When the English battery was ready to open fire Hebecourt saw that further resistance was useless and lighting a slow match to the magazine the French escaped down the lake in their boats and a few hours later an explosion which hurled one bastion of old Fort Carrillon skyward shook the promontory. Thus did French Carillon become English Ticonderoga and "Ticonderoga 1758-9" should be among the battle honours to be borne on the colours of the Black Watch. It is true that these honorary distinctions are awarded by the King only in case of victory but Ticonderoga 1758-9 would certainly be as much a victory as "South Africa 1899-1902," which has been granted. South Africa was not all victory and the Black Watch suffered at Magersfontein as it did at Ticonderoga under Abercrombie.

The length of time elapsed since the battle would also be no objection to the honor being now granted as it was not until 1910, two and one half centuries later that the armies that upheld British honour on the Coast of Morocco were authorized to bear "Tangier 1662-1680" on their colours and appointments.

Ticonderoga is the one place on the American continent where Great Britain and France, Canada and the United States can all unite on one common ground. The Yankees and British can meet here and clasp hands over the time when they once fought together and there is not even a sectional feeling which detracts from the unanimity. The North, South, East and West of the United States all join with equal fervour. Each nation had its defeats here at different times but each also had its victories. Therefore there is no battle honour which could be conferred on any British regiment that would please more people of different nations than "Ticonderoga 1758-9." The fact that there is at present in the village of Ticonderoga a public library and historical building dedicated to a British Regiment, even though this same regiment in its line of duty fought against us in a later war, is sufficient proof that we consider Ticonderoga of international history and above matters of local prejudice.

The rest of the story is soon told. Crown Point was captured and the army was to have moved forward to Isleoux-Noix and to the St. Lawrence but a succession of storms so delayed operations that further active movements were abandoned for the remainder of the season. Amherst profiting by the fatal precipitation of his predecessor was slow but sure and in this campaign was successful in every enterprise that he undertook.

After the capture of Crown Point the army under Amherst was mainly employed in building operations on Lake Champlain, Fort Amherst at Crown Point and Fort Ticonderoga in place of old Fort Carrillon at Ticonderoga. The Black Watch was stationed at Crown Point and helped to build Fort Amherst.

In November, they went into camp for the winter and in his report of *Garrisons and Winter Quarters of His Majesty's forces in North America under the command of His Excellency, Major General Amherst, Headquarters at New York, 15 Dec., 1759* in the Public Record Office, the stations of the Black Watch were as follows: 1st Battalion Royal Highland Regiment, 1 company Halfway Brook, 5 companies Fort Edward, 1 company Fort Miller, 1 company Saratoga, 1 company Stillwater and 1 company Halfmoon, 2nd Battalion Royal Highland Regiment, Albany, one Battalion of the Inniskilling (27th Foot) and two companies of the Rangers were left at Crown Point, six companies Late

Brig. Gen'l Forbe's (17th Foot) at Ticonderoga, and four companies 17th Foot at Fort George.

The following season (1760) the Black Watch was with Amherst at the capture of Montreal which was the end of the French domain on the American Continent.

In 1761 the Black Watch with ten regiments embarked for Barbados there to join an armament against Martinique and Havana. After the surrender of Havana, the first battalion of the 42nd and Montgomery's Highlanders embarked for New York which they reached in the end of October, 1762. Before leaving Cuba most of the second battalion of the 42nd fit for service were consolidated with the first, and the remainder shipped to Scotland where they were reduced the following year.

The Black Watch was stationed at Albany until the summer of 1763, when they, with a detachment of Montgomery's Highlanders and another of the 60th, under command of Col. Henry Boquet were sent to the relief of Fort Pitt then besieged by the Indians. The 42nd passed the winter at Fort Pitt and during the summer of 1764, eight companies were sent with the army of Boquet against the Ohio Indians. After subduing the Indians they returned to Fort Pitt, January 1765. The regiment remained in Pennsylvania until the month of July, 1767, when it embarked at Philadelphia for Ireland. Such of the men who preferred to remain in America were permitted to join other regiments. These volunteers were so numerous that along with those who had been previously sent home disabled and others discharged and settled in America, the regiment that returned was very small in proportion to that which had left Scotland.

CHAPTER 5

Major Duncan Campbell

Let us now turn our attention to Major Duncan
Campbell as not only would no sketch of the Black Watch
of Ticonderoga be complete without the legend with
which his name is associated, but we are perhaps more
interested in him than any other officer of the Regiment of that time because he lies buried in the cemetery
midway between Hudson Falls (formerly Sandy Hill)
and Fort Edward. The other officers and men who were
killed July 8, 1758, were doubtless buried on the field of
battle and if the graves were ever marked, these marks
have long since been destroyed.

No ghost story is more widely known or better au-
thenticated than that of Duncan Campbell of Inverawe.
The following is taken from Parkman's "Montcalm and
Wolfe" and is the story as was told by Dean Stanley and
endorsed by the family of the hero of the tale:

> The ancient castle of Inverawe stands by the banks
> of the Awe, in the midst of the wild and picturesque
> scenery of the Western Highlands.
>
> Late one evening, before the middle of the last
> century, as the laird, Duncan Campbell, sat alone in
> the old hall, there was a loud knocking at the gate;

and, opening it, he saw a stranger, with torn clothing and kilt besmeared with blood, who in a breathless voice begged for asylum. He went on to say that he had killed a man in a fray, and that the pursuers were at his heels. Campbell promised to shelter him.

"Swear on your dirk!" said the stranger; and Campbell swore.

He then led him to a secret recess in, the depths of the castle. Scarcely was he hidden when again there was a loud knocking at the gate, and two armed men appeared.

"Your cousin Donald has been murdered, and we are looking for the murderer!"

Campbell, remembering his oath, professed to have no knowledge of the fugitive; and the men went on their way. The laird, in great agitation, lay down to rest in a large dark room where at length he fell asleep. Waking suddenly in bewilderment and terror, he saw the ghost of the murdered Donald standing by his bedside, and heard a hollow voice pronounce the words:

"Inverawe! Inverawe! blood has been shed. Shield not the murderer."

In the morning Campbell went to the hiding place of the guilty man and told him that he could harbour him no longer.

"You have sworn on your dirk" he replied; and the laird of Inverawe, greatly perplexed and troubled, made a compromise between conflicting duties, promised not to betray his guest, led him to the neighbouring mountain—Ben Cruachan—and hid him in a cave.

In the next night, as he lay tossing in feverish slumbers, the same stern voice awoke him, the ghost of his cousin Donald stood again at his bedside, and again he heard the same appalling words:

"Inverawe! Inverawe! blood has been shed. Shield not the murderer!"

At break of day he hastened, in strange agitation, to the cave; but it was empty, the stranger had gone. At night, as he strove in vain to sleep, the vision appeared once more, ghastly pale, but less stern of aspect than before.

"Farewell, Inverawe!" it said; "Farewell, till we meet at *Ticonderoga!*"

The strange name dwelt in Campbell's memory. He had joined the Black Watch, or Forty-Second Regiment, then employed in keeping order in the turbulent Highlands. In time he became its major; and, a year or two after the war broke out, he went with it to America. Here, to his horror, he learned that it was ordered to the attack of Ticonderoga. His story was well known among his brother officers. They combined among themselves to disarm his fears; and when they reached the fatal spot they told him on the eve of the battle, "This is not Ticonderoga; we are not there yet; this is Fort George."[1] But in the morning he came to them with haggard looks.

"I have seen him! You have deceived me! He came to my tent last night! This is Ticonderoga! I shall die today!" and his prediction was fulfilled.

As will be seen by the preceding pages, Inverawe lived

---

1. More probably Fort Carrillon.

nine days after the battle and was not even mortally wounded if it had been possible in those times to have had antiseptic treatment, but the real point of the legend is that he had been warned of Ticonderoga when he did not know there was such a place, years before there was any prospect of his being sent there and when Ticonderoga was only the Indian name for a point of land on a lake in the wilderness of a far off continent.

To one interested no place could be more fascinating than old Inverawe[1] everything connected with it breathes of legend and romance and naturally this was one of the first places visited in our Black Watch pilgrimage last summer. Taynuilt, the railroad station nearest Inverawe is a small village across the Awe and about a mile away as the crow flies, but to drive to our destination, one must follow the road two miles up the River to the old bridge which was being built at the time that the Major left for the war in America in 1756. The builder was Captain William Pitman apparently a good friend of Duncan of Inverawe as he charged him with the safe keeping during his absence of his daughter Janet and his favourite dog. History does not record what happened to the dog but the Captain married the daughter and in time Inverawe became her property.

After crossing the Awe the road turns down the north side of the River and winds through a magnificent park, some of the trees of which must certainly have been there before the Major's time. This is all the more remarkable because with the exception of the parks of the private estates, Scotland is nearly a treeless country and even the

---

1. Inver means "the mouth of," therefore the mouth of the River Awe.

mountains and wild land which with us would be covered
with forests, have there only grass and heather. Then at
the end of a delightful four mile drive was old Inverawe
house and a most cordial and hospitable welcome from its
present owner.

The old house has had many additions in the past one
hundred and fifty years but the entrance hall and the main
part of the building and particularly the room where Duncan Campbell saw the ghost, are still very much as they
were in his time. We endeavoured to learn as much as possible of the family history of the Campbells of Inverawe,
but like the records of the Black Watch of that time, there
was in 1910, little left but tradition.

Appendices

Appendix A

Roll of Officers of the 42nd Highlanders

New York, May 22, 1757
from an Old Paper in Possession of
the 7th Duke of Atholl

Lt. Col. Francis Grant, son of the Laird of Grant, wounded at Ticonderoga.

Major Duncan Campbell, of Inverawe, killed at Ticonderoga.

Captain Gordon Graham, of Drainie, wounded at Ticonderoga.

Captain John Reid, of Straloch, wounded at Martinique.

Captain John NcNeil.

Captain Allan Campbell, son of Barcaldine.

Captain Thomas Graeme, of Duchray, wounded at Ticonderoga.

Captain James Abercrombie.

Captain John Campbell, of Strachur, wounded at Ticonderoga.

Captain John Campbell, of Duneavis, killed at Ticonderoga.

Lieutenant William Grant, of Rothiemurchus family, wounded at Ticonderoga.

Lieutenant Robert Gray, wounded at Ticonderoga.

Lieutenant John Campbell, younger of Glenyon, wounded at Ticonderoga.[1]

Lieutenant George Farquharson, son of Farquharson of Micris, Braemar, killed at Ticonderoga.

Lieutenant Sir James Cockburn.[2]

Lieutenant Kenneth Tolmie.

Lieutenant James Grant (Adjutant), wounded at Ticonderoga.

Lieutenant John Graham (quartermaster) wounded at Ticonderoga and wounded at Fort Pitt.

Lieutenant Hugh McPherson, killed at Ticonderoga.

Lieutenant Alex. Turnbull, of Strathcavere, wounded at Martinique.

Lieutenant Alex. Campbell, son of Inverawe, wounded at Ticonderoga.

Lieutenant Alex. McIntosh, wounded at Ticonderoga.

---

1. Major Sir Duncan Campbell of Bacaldine says should be 'of Glendaruel' and that younger of Glenlyon went to the Marines in 1755.
2. Lieut. Sir James Cockburn transferred to 48th Foot. Ensign Patrick Balneavis made Lieut., commission dated 1st April, 1758, and Mr. Elbert Hering succeeded to the Ensigncy, commission dated April 3rd, 1758.

Lieutenant James Gray.

Lieutenant William Baillie, killed at Ticonderoga.

Lieutenant Hugh Arnot.

Lieutenant John Sutherland, killed at Ticonderoga.

Lieutenant John Small.

Lieutenant Archibald Campbell.

Lieutenant James Campbell.

Lieutenant Archibald Lament.

Ensign Duncan Campbell, wounded at Fort Pitt.

Ensign Patrick Balnea viz.,[1] son of Edradour, wounded at Ticonderoga, wounded at Martinique.

Ensign Patrick Stewart,[2] son of Bonskeid, killed at Ticonderoga.

Ensign Norman MacLeod.

Ensign George Campbell.

Ensign Donald Campbell.

Ensign James McIntosh, wounded at Fort Pitt.

Ensign Alex. McIntosh, wounded at Martinique.

Ensign Peter Grant, wounded at Ticonderoga.

Three additional Companies embarked for America, November, 1757.

Captain James Stewart, younger of Urrard, wounded at Ticonderoga.

---

1. See footnote at bottom of preceding page.
2. Miss Ethel Lomas, copyist at Public Record Office London is authority for the statement that this should be Peter (not Patrick) Stewart.

Captain James Murray, son of Lord G. Murray, wounded at Ticonderoga, wounded at Martinique.

Captain Thomas Stirling, younger of Ardoch, wounded at Martinique, wounded at New Jersey.

Lieutenant Simon Blair.

Lieutenant David Barclay, killed at Martinique.

Lieutenant Archibald Campbell, wounded at Ticonderoga.

Lieutenant Alex. Mackay.

Lieutenant Alex. Menzies.

Lieutenant David Milne,[3] wounded at Ticonderoga, wounded at Martinique.

Ensign Duncan Stewart, son of Derculich.

Ensign George Rattray, son of Dalralzion, killed at Ticonderoga.

Ensign Alex. Farquharson.

Ensign John Smith is added in ink to the 1858 Army List in the N.Y. State Library at Albany and is also marked as "wounded at Ticonderogra."

---

3. This name is given as David Mills in the Army List, but the Duke of Atholl is authority for the statement that Milne is correct.

APPENDIX B

Roll of Capt. John Reid's Company, November 1757

The following is the roll of Capt. John Reid's Company of the 42nd, which was commanded by Capt. James Murray during the expedition. Taken from Atholl Records, page 440, Vol. III. This roll was made out at the muster in October, 1757, and contains the names of those who served in the Company for the previous six months. Unfortunately the names of the non-commissioned officers and men who were wounded at Ticonderoga are not shown.

Capt. James Murray, wounded.

Lieut. David Mill, wounded.

Lieut. Kenneth Tolmie.

Ensign Charles Menzies.

Sergt. Alex'r Gumming.

Sergt. James McNab.

Sergt. John McAndrews.

Sergt. John Watson.

Corporal Jonathan Grant.

Corporal John Gumming.

Corporal Angus McDonald

Corporal John Stewart.

Drum Alan Campbell.

Drum Walter McIntyre, killed.

PRIVATES

Wm. Anderson.

John Buchanan, killed.

Angus Cameron.

Hugh Cameron, killed.

Wm. Carmichael.

Donald Carr, killed.

Hugh Christie.

James Farquharson, killed.

Alex Fraser.

John Forbes.Donald Fraser.

Donald Fraser.

Hugh Fraser.

Hugh Fraser, killed.

John Graham.

Donald Grant.

James Grant.

John Grant.

John Grant.

William Grant.

James Gordon.

William Gordon.

Alex. Gumming.

Donald Kennedy.

Donald Kennedy.

John Kennedy.

George McAdam.

John McArthur.

Donald McColl.

Donald McDiarmid.

Angus McDonald.

Arch'd McDonald.

Arch'd McDonald, killed.

James McDonald, killed.

John McDonald.

Lachlan McDonald.

William McDonald, killed.

Neil McEachern.

Peter McFarlane.

Peter McFarlane, killed.

John McGillvray.

Leonard McGlashan.

Alex McGregor.

Donald McGregor.

Robert McGregor.

John McIntosh.

Alex McIntyre.

Donald McIntyre.

James McIntyre, killed.

Hector McInven.

Hugh McKay.

Alex'r McKenzie.

Hugh McKenzie.

John McKenzie, killed.

John McKenzie.

Roderick McKenzie.

Dougall McLachlan, killed.

John McLaren.
Roderick McLaren.
Neil McLeod.
Norman McLeod, killed.
Donald McLeish.
Donald McLeish.
William McLinnion.
Neil McMillan.
Donald McNeil, killed.
Neil McNeil.
Hugh McPhee.
John McPhee.
Alex McPherson.
Donald McPherson.
Donald McQueen, killed.
James Michael.
Donald Murray.
James Murray.
James Rea.
Alex'r Reid.
Alex'r Ross.
Donald Ross.
Hugh Ross, killed.
John Ross.
Donald Robertson.
Neil Shaw.

John Sinclair, died of wounds.
John Smith.
Walter Spaulding.
Alex'r Stewart.
Charles Stewart, died of wounds,
Donald Stewart, died of wounds.
Walter Stewart, died of wounds .
Robert Urquhart.
Donald Watson.
Donald Wheet.
William Wishart.
Duncan Wright.

Roll of Capt. James Murray's Company, November 1757

This Company was at Fort Edward captained by Capt. James Abercrombie and not in the battle of July 8, 1758. From Atholl Records, p. 431, Vol. III.

Sergt. Wm. Grant.
Sergt. Charles Robinson.
Sergt, John McQueen.
Corporal John Leslie.
Corporal Robert Lachlan.
Drummer Alan Campbell.

PRIVATES

George Bremmer.
Donald Brown.
Duncan Cameron.
John Campbell.
Donald Conacher.
William Cowie.
James Douglas.

Donald Drummond.
James Duncan.
Alex Fraser (1).
Alex Fraser (2).
William Fife.
Robert Grant.
Alex Irvine.
James Kennedy.
Duncan McAndrew.
Donald McDiarmid.
Archibald McDonald.
Archibald McDonald.
Donald McDonald.
John McDonald.
William McDonald.

Peter McFarlane.
Alex'r McIntosh.
Robert McIntosh.
Robert McIntosh.
William McIntosh.
Donald McLean.
Donald McLean.
Thos. McNab.
Alex McPherson.
James McPherson.
Donald McRaw.
Robert Menzies.
William Munroe.
John Murray.
Alex'r Nicholson.
Alex'r Norrie.
Alex'r Reid.
Alex'r Robertson.
Angus Robertson.
Archibald Robertson.
Charles Robertson.
Donald Robertson.
James Robertson.
James Robertson.
John Robertson.
Peter Robertson.
James Scroggie.

Alex'r Stewart.
Alex'r Stewart.
Alex'r Stewart.
John Stewart.
Robert Stewart.
Thomas Stewart.
William Stewart.
John Wighton.
John Wighton.

Black Watch Losses at Ticonderoga Compared With Those of Other Wars

In the *Regimental Losses in the American Civil War, 1861-1865*, a treatise in the extent and nature of the mortuary losses in the Union Regiments, with full and exhaustive statistics compiled from the official records on file on the State Military Bureaus and at Washington, by William F. Fox, Lieut. Col. U. S. V., the writer states that he has examined the records of 2,000 regiments of the Union Army and on page 2 he says:

> The one regiment in all the Union Army which sustained the greatest loss in battle during the American Civil War was the 5th New Hampshire Infantry. It lost 295 men, killed or mortally wounded in action during the four years of service from 1861 to 1865. It served in the first division, second corps. This division was commanded successively by General Richardson, Hancock, Caldwall, Barlow and Miles and any regiment that followed the fortunes of these men was sure to find plenty of bloody work cut out for it. Its loss includes 18 officers killed, a number far in excess of the usual proportions and indicates that the men were bravely led.

There were 34 regiments of the Union Army whose casualties in killed, wounded or missing amounted to 58 per cent or over of the men engaged in one battle in each case, however, there was not a full regiment engaged. For example, the 1st Minnesota at Gettysburg, which was the highest percentage, had 47 killed and 168 wounded, or a total loss of 215 out of 262 men engaged. This is a loss of 82 per cent.

The 9th Illinois at Shiloh had 61 killed, 300 wounded and 5 missing, a total of 63.3 per cent.

The Light Brigade which has been immortalized by Tennyson took 673 officers and men into that charge at Balaklava in which 113 were killed and 134 wounded, a total of 247 or 36.7 per cent.

The heaviest loss in the German army of the Franco-Prussian war was the 16th Infantry (3rd Westphalian) at Mars la Tour which had 509 killed, 619 wounded, 365 missing, a total of 1,484 or 49.4 per cent, out of 3,000 men. The regiments of the German army had 3,000 men.

The above are the greatest casualties suffered in three great wars taken from a book compiled by an authority who had made a study of the subject. Compare with these the loss of the Black Watch at Ticonderoga given by Col. Stewart of Garth as 8 officers, 9 sergeants and 297 men killed and 17 officers, 10 sergeants and 306 soldiers wounded or a casualty of 647 (64.7 per cent) out of the 1,000 men of the 42nd reported by General Abercrombie at Lake George, June 29, 1758.

Table of Losses of Black Watch in the Seven Year War

The loss sustained by the regiment during the seven years it was employed in America and the West Indies was as follows:

	KILLED						WOUNDED					
	Field Officers	Captains	Subalterns	Serjeants	Drummers	Privates	Field Officers	Captains	Subalterns	Serjeants	Drummers	Privates
Ticonderoga, July 8, 1758	1	1	6	9	2	297		5	12	10		306
Martinique, January, 1759						8			1	2		22
Gaudeloupe, Feb. and Mar., 1759			1	1		25			4	3		57
General Amherst's Expedition to the Lakes, July and Aug., 1759						3					1	4
Martinique, Jan. and Feb., 1762	1	1	6			12	1	1	7	3	1	72
Havana, June and July, 1762, both battalions						6				1		12
Expedition under Colonel Boquet, August, 1763		1	1	1		26		1	1	2	2	30
Second Expedition under Boquet, in 1764 and 1765						7				1		19
Total in the Seven Years' War	1	3	9	12	2	384	1	7	25	22	4	522

Stewart of Garth, Appendix.

Official Titles of Black Watch at Different Periods

1667 to 1739, The Black Watch.

1739 to 1749, The Regiment was known during this period by the names of its Colonels, as was the custom in the British Army at that time, Earl of Crawford's, Lord Sempill's, Lord John Murray's. It was also called The Highland Regiment. It is said that the Regiment was at first the 43rd Regt. of Foot, but while it was 43rd in order of precedence it is a questionable whether it was ever officially called the 43rd.

1749 to 1758, 42nd Regiment of Foot (The Highland Regiment) .

1758 to 1861, 42nd (or Royal Highland) Regiment of Foot.

1861 to 1881, 42nd Royal Highlanders (The Black Watch).

1881 to date, 1st Battalion The Black Watch (Royal Highlanders).

1758 to 1786, 2nd Battalion 42nd (or Royal Highland), Regiment of Foot.

1786 to 1862, 73rd (Highland) Regiment of Foot.

1862 to 1881, 73d (Perthshire) Regiment of Foot.

1881 to date, 2nd Battalion The Black Watch (Royal Highlanders).

Appendix G
Principal Campaigns, Battles, Etc.

*=Honours on the Colours, the figures showing the Battalion concerned.

1743-47 Flanders.
1745 Fontenoy.
1745 Jacobite rising.
1757-60 Canada.
1758 Ticonderoga.
1759 Guadeloupe.
1762 Martinique.
1762 Havannah.
1762-67 Indian Frontier.
1763 Bushy Run.
1775-81 America.
1776 Long Island.
1776 White Plains.
1776 Brooklyn.
1776 Fort Washington.
1777 Pisquata.
1777 Brandy wine.

1777 Germantown.
1778 Freehold.
1780 Charlestown.
1783 Mysore* (2).
1783 Mangalore* (2).
1793 Pondicherry.
1793 Nieuport. 1794 Nimeguen.
1795 Ceylon.
1795 Guildermalsen.
1796 St. Lucia.
1797 St.Vincent.
1798 Minorca.
1799 Seringapatam* (2)
1799 Genoa.
1799 Cadiz.
1800 Malta.

1801 Egypt★ (1).

1801 Alexandria.

1801 Aboukir.

1801 Mandora.

1808-14 Peninsula★ (1).

1808 Roleia.

1808 Vimiera.

1809 Corunna★ (1).

1810 Busaco.

1811 Fuentes d'Onor★ (1).

1812 Ciudad Rodrigo.

1812 Salamanca.

1812 Burgos.

1813 Pyrenees★ (1).

1813 Gohrde.

1813 Nivelle★ (1).

1813 Nive★ (1).

1814 Orthes★ (1).

1814 Antwerp.

1814 Toulouse★ (1).

1815 Quatre Bras.

1815 Waterloo★ (1 and 2)

1815 Netherlands.

1846-53 South Africa★ (2),

1854 Alma★ (1).

1854 Balaclava.

1854 Kertch.

1855 Yenikale.

1855 Sevastopol★ (1).

1857-58 Indian Mutiny.

1857 Cawnpore.

1858 Lucknow★ (1).

1874 Ashantee★ (1).

1882-84 Egypt★ (1).

1882 Tel-el-Kebir★ (1).

1884-85 Nile★ (1).

1884 El-Teb.

1884 Tamai.

1885 Kirbekan★ (1).

1893-95 Flanders.

1899-1902 South Africa★.

1900 Paardeberg★.

Appendix H

British Regiments at Ticonderoga 1758

With Notes from Farmer's Regimental Records

27th

1751-1881, The 27th (Inniskilling) Regiment of Foot. Also 1758 "Lord Blakeney's."

1881 (from) First Battalion "The Royal Inniskilling Fusiliers." Nickname "The Lumps."

Notes. Formed from three Companies of the Inniskilling forces. It is unique in using the old Irish war-pipes. While employed on the Isthmus of Darien all but nine of six hundred men succumbed. For distinguished gallantry at St. Lucia, in 1696, it was directed that the French garrison in marching out should lay down their arms to the 27th, other marks of favour being likewise accorded to the officers and men of the regiment.

42ND

1749-58, 42nd Regiment of Foot (The Highland Regiment).

1758-1861, 42nd (or Royal Highland) Regiment of Foot. Also "Lord John Murray's," 1758 and 59.

1881 (from) 1st Battalion The Black Watch (Royal Highlanders).

Regimental Badges "The Royal Cypher within the Garter." The badge and motto of the Order of the Thistle. Also (in each of the four corners) the Royal Cypher ensigned with the Imperial Crown. Also "The Spinx" (for Egypt, 1801).

Notes. The 1st Battalion of this famous corps, the oldest Highland regiment in the British army, was raised from six Independent companies of Highlanders. Its sombre dress of black, blue, and green tartan gave rise to its popular name. To enumerate its services is simply to narrate the military history of Great Britain since the early part of the last century. Hardly a campaign has been conducted, or a battle fought, in which the Black Watch—one battalion or the other, or both in company—has not participated; always with bravery, and frequently with conspicuous gallantry. Thereto its records of services abundantly testifies. At Fontenoy, Ticonderoga, and at Bushy Run "extraordinary and unexampled" gallantry was shown. It received Royal distinction in its change of title in 1758, and was privileged to wear the red heckle in the

bonnet, in recognition of its conduct at the battle
of Guildermalsen in 1795. In Egypt (in 1801, for
which it bears "The Sphinx"), before Alexandria,
it captured the Standard of the French Invincible
Legion. Since then it has heaped fame on fame,
and added honour to honour on its colours. Nor
has the 2nd Battalion (raised in Perthshire in
1758 as the second Battalion of the 42nd, but,
renumbered, long known as the 73rd prior to
the territorial restoration of the ancient status)
failed to win fresh laurels as occasion arose. At
Mangalore (1783) against Tippoo Sahib, and side
by side with the senior Battalion at Waterloo,
in the Netherlands, in the Indian Mutiny, and
in the Kaffir wars of 1846-53, it has worthily
sustained the undying fame of the regiment.
Recent events in South Africa show that neither
the officers nor the men of today have lost one
iota of that traditional dash, determination, and
the bravery which have won for the Black Watch
so glorious a place in British military annals.

44TH

1751-82, The 44th Regiment of Foot. Also 1758,
"General Abercrombie's."

1881 (from) The First Battalion "The Essex
Regiment."

Nicknames. "The Two Fours" (of the 44th). "The
Little Fighting Fours," (the regiment saw hard
service in the Peninsula, and its men were of

small average stature). "The Pompadours" and "Saucy Pompeys." (Tradition relates that when the facings were changed in 1764 (the crimson not wearing well) the Colonel desired Blue, but the authorities objecting, he chose Purple, a favourite colour of Madame de Pompadour, a mistress of Louis XV, of France).

Note. The 44th captured an Eagle of the 62nd French Infantry at Salamanica.

46TH

1751-82, The 46th Regiment of Foot. Also 1758 "Lieut. Gen. Thomas Murray's."

1881 (from) Second Battalion "Duke of Cornwall's Light infantry."

Nicknames. These pertain to the late 46th; "Murray's Buck's" (from Colonel name (1743-64) and its smart appearance on home duty in Scottish Royal livery). "The Surprisers" (from an incident (1777) in the American War). "The Lacedemonians" (its Colonel once when under fire, made a disciplinarian speech concerning the Lacedemonians). Also in early days, "The Edinburgh Regiment." "The Red Feathers." "The Docs" (the initials) .

Note. "The Two Feathers" is a distinction of the 46th, a Light company of which, in 1777, with others were brigaded as "The Light Battalion." The Americans were so harassed by the Brigade that they vowed "No Quarter." In derision, to prevent mistakes, the Light Battalion dyed their feathers red; the 46th Foot alone has retained the distinction.

55TH

1757-82, The 55th Regiment of Foot. Also "Lord Howe's" in 1858 and "Prideaux's" in 1759.

1881 (from) Second Battalion "The Border Regiment."

Nickname. "The Two Fives" (to the 55th for its number).

Note. The Dragon of China is on the Regimental Badge of the 55th in honour of the victorious campaign in China in 1840-42.

1ST AND 4TH BATTALIONS 60TH

1755-57, The 62nd (Royal American) Regiment of Foot; renumbered.

1757-1824, The 60th (Royal American) Regiment of Foot. 1881 (from) Second Battalion "The Border Regiment."

Notes. This regiment, though possessing no Colours, bears more honours than any other regiment, the Highland Light Infantry coming next with twenty-nine. Motto, "Swift and Bold," bestowed according to tradition by General Wolfe in recognition of its conduct at Quebec.

80TH

1758-64, The 80th (Light-armed) Regiment of Foot. Also "Gage's." (Disbanded 1764).

The Royal Regiment of Artillery.

One arm or other of this branch of the Service has, obviously, taken part in every campaign; a particularized list is therefore unnecessary. The guns are the Colours of the Artillery, and as such are entitled to all "parade honours." Formerly, regimental honours appear to have been worn by certain companies. Amongst such are Niagara, Leipzig, Waterloo, and The Dragon of China.

Nicknames. "The Gunners;" "The Four-wheeled Hussars" (of the Royal Horse Artillery).

Notes. Trains of artillery seem to have been raised in the time of Henry VIII,; and up to 1716 appear to have been disbanded after each campaign. In 1716 several companies received permanent corporate existence, since which exigencies of modern warfare have led to an enormous increase in the number of batteries. But from first to last, the record of the Royal Artillery has been one of distinction, and it may fitly be said to share the honours of all other regiments. The Royal Irish Artillery were absorbed in 1801, and the East India Company's Artillery in 1858.

British Regiments at Ticonderoga 1759

1ST

1751-1812, The 1st, or The Royal Regiment of Foot, also the "Royals."

1881 (from) The Royal Scots (Lothian Regiment).

Nickname. "Pontius Pilate's Body-Guard." It is a legend of the Regiment that the Romans carried off a number of wild, war-like Highlanders as prisoners after their conquest of Britain, and these men and their descendants became soldiers of the Roman Empire and as such they guarded the tomb of Our Saviour after the crucifixion. This Scottish company, for it only consisted of one hundred men under a centurion, was kept distinct from the Roman Army proper. At the time of the crucifixion they were called Pontius Pilate's Scots Guards, and their descendants were the nucleus of the First Royal Scots in later years.

Notes. The oldest Regiment of Foot in the British Army. Traditionally regarded as the ancient bodyguard of the Scottish kings, this famous corps was in the service of Sweden, as "Hepburn's Regiment," from 1625 to 1633; and in that of France from 1633 to 1678, when (under Dumbarton) it came to England. It received its title in 1684 in recognition of the capture of a Colour from the Moors at Tangier. At Sedgemoor (1685) it also captured the Duke of Monmouth's Standard.

17TH

1751-82, The 17th Regiment of Foot. Also "Forbes."

1881 (from) "The Leicestershire Regiment."

Nicknames. "The Bengal Tigers" (from its badge); "The Lily-whites" (from its facings).

Notes. Mainly raised near London; twelve regiments in all were formed in 1688, but this and the 16th (The Bedfordshire) are alone in commission now.

77TH.

1756-63, The 77th (Montgomery Highlanders) Regiment; disbanded 1763.

27TH, 42ND, 55TH, 80TH & ROYAL ARTILLERY

See appendix H, Ticonderoga, 1758.

Provincial Regiments
at Ticonderoga

The writer will have to admit that this list is incomplete, even the N.Y. State Library at Albany had only scattered items

1758

The *New York Colonial Manuscripts*, edited by Callaghan, page 732, in the list of regiments having officers wounded at the battle of July 8, 1758, gives the following regiments: Col. DeLanceys, New York; Col. Babcock's, Rhode Island; Col. Fitche's, Connecticut; Col. Worcester's, Connecticut; Col. Bagley's, Massachusetts; Col. Partridge's, Massachusetts; Col. Preble's, Massachusetts; Col. Johnston's, New Jersey. Parkmen mentions Col. Bradstreet with his regiment of boatmen, armed and drilled as soldiers and it is also certain that Roger's Rangers were with the expedition.

The year book of the Maine Chapter of the Society of Colonial Wars for 1900 gives much information in regard to Col. Preble's regiment, Maine being in 1758 a part of Massachusetts. Mention is made in this article of regiments officered by Col. Doty, Col. Joseph Williams, Col. Nickols, Col. Whiting.

Also in the *New York Colonial Manuscripts*, Vol. 10, P. 827 it mentions a force of about 3,000 men nearly all of whom were provincials, under Col. Bradstreet, in the expedition against Fort Frontinac after the battle of July 8, 1758, and of the number of soldiers engaged, the list is given as New Yorkers 1112, Col. Williams' regiment 413, Col. Douty's 248, Rhode Island 318, and Jersey 418.

It is not clear whether these regiments were at the battle of Ticonderoga and were not mentioned in list page 732 of the *New York Colonial Manuscripts* because none of the officers were wounded, or whether they were the same regiments but with different officers, a change having been made after the battle.

1759

The provincial regiments mentioned in Commissary Wilson's Orderly Book as being in the Ticonderoga expedition of 1759 are as follows: Col. Lyman's, Connecticut; Col. Whiting's, Connecticut; Col. Worcester's, Connecticut; Col. Fitch's, Connecticut; Col. Willard's, Massachusetts; Col. Ruggle's, Massachusetts; Col. Lovell's, New Hampshire; Col. Schuyler's, New Jersey; Col. Babcock's, Rhode Island.

Appendix K

Biographical Sketches of Some of the Officers of 1758

James Abercrombie

James Abercrombie was promoted to a captaincy in the 42nd or 1st Battalion of the Royal Highlanders on the 16th of February, 1756. On the 5th of May, 1759, he was appointed aid-de-camp to Maj. Gen. Amherst, with whom he made the campaigns of that and the following year. On the 25th of July, 1760, he was appointed Major of the 78th or Eraser's Highlanders and in September following was employed by Gen. Amherst in communicating to the Marquis de Vaudreuil the conditions preparatory to the surrender of Montreal and in obtaining the signature of that governor to them. (Knox's Journal). The 78th having been disbanded in 1763, Major Abercrombie retired on half pay. On the 27th of March, 1770, he again entered active service as Lt. Colonel of the 22nd Regiment then serving in America under the command of Lt. Col. Gage and was killed in the memorable Battle of Bunker Hill on the 17th of June, 1775[*].

---

[*] From *New York Colonial Manuscripts* by Broadhead, Weed, Parsons Co., Albany, 1856, page 160.

HUGH ARNOT

Hugh Arnot was taken from the half pay list and appointed a Lieutenant in the 42nd Highlanders, 9th April, 1756, at the augmentation of that Regiment on its coming to America, and was promoted to a Company on the 27th December, 1757. He served in the unfortunate affair of Ticonderoga in 1758, and in 1759 accompanied Amherst as above. On the 16th August, 1760, he exchanged into the 46th Foot, in which Regiment he continued to serve until 1769, when his name was dropped from the Army List[*].

---

[*] From Wilson's Orderly Book, p. 143.

PATRICK BALNEAVES

Patrick Balneaves, of Edradour, entered the 42nd, as Ensign, 28th January, 1756, and was promoted to be Lieutenant 1st April, 1758; he was wounded at Ticonderoga, 1758; and again at Martinico in 1762; became Captain-Lieutenant 23rd August, 1763, and left the army in 1770[*].

---

[*] From Stewart. Army Lists. *N.Y. Colonial Manuscripts*, p. 729, Vol. 10.

ALLAN CAMPBELL

Allan Campbell, son of Barcaldine, entered the Army as Ensign of the 43rd (now the 42nd) Highlanders, Dec. 25, 1744, and served that year against the Pretender. Was made prisoner of war at Preston Pans, 21st September 1745 and sent on parole to Perth. Was appointed lieutenant Dec. 1, 1746. He obtained a Company 13th of May, 1755, and the next year came to America, where he shared the difficulties and honours of the Regiment. In June, 1759, he was appointed Major for the campaign under Amherst, and was actively employed at the Head of the Grenadiers and Rangers, clearing the way for the army up the Lakes. He became major in the army 15th August, 1762, and went on half pay on the reduction of the regiment in 1763, having obtained a grant of 5,000 acres of land at Crown Point. He served 19 years in the regiment. In 1770, he was appointed Major of the 36th or Herefordshire Foot, then serving in Jamaica; became Lieutenant-Colonel in the army in May (1772), and of his regiment in January, 1778; Colonel in the Army, 17th November 1780; Major-General in 1787; and died 1795. His Regiment did not serve in America during the Revolutionary War[*].

An extract from his will dated 2nd March 1787, reads:

> And whereas I am under a grant from the Crown intitled to a considerable tract of land and *heredits situate*, lying and being in the Province of New York in the County of Albany in America, between Ticonderoga and Crown Point. I do hereby give, devise and bequeath unto my two sisters, Isabella Campbell, (wife of John C. of Archalader, in the Shire of Perth, in North Britain, aforesaid Esquire), and Jane Campbell of Edinchip, in the Shire of Perth, aforesaid, widow of Colin Campbell of Edinchip, aforesaid, Esq. deceased, their heirs, executors, Administrators, and Assigns, all my said track of land and *heredits*, in America. . . .

---

[*] From Browne, IV, 150. Knox Journal, I, 373, 377, 387; II. 401. Army List. Commissionary Wilson's Orderly Book. 1759 p. 18. Stewart of Garth Appendix.

ARCHIBALD CAMPBELL

Archibald Campbell. Born 1720. Eldest son of Duncan Campbell of Glendaruel and Lockhead. His mother was Elizabeth, daughter of the Rev. Archibald Campbell of Inverary. He was appointed Ensign 42nd Regt. 23d Jan. 1756, Lieut. 28th July 1757, Captain 4th Dec. 1759
Died 3rd June 1762.

DONALD CAMPBELL

Donald Campbell, son of Donald Campbell Bailie of McKairn, Taynuilt Argyll, was appointed Ensign in the 42nd Regt. of Foot, 5th May 1756. He was with one of the additional companies in the *Anandall* which sprang two leaks, lost her mizzen mast, was attacked three times by Privateers (which they beat off with small arms), and was driven into the West Indies, so that she did not arrive in New York, in time for the company to join the attack on Ticonderoga. He was appointed Lieut. 24th July 1758 and retired 13th June 1761, having served with the Royal Highlanders from 1758 to 1761[*].

---

[*] From *Highlanders in America* by MacLean, page 176, N.Y. Colonial Documents, page 629.

DUNCAN CAMPBELL

Killochronan, Island of Mull.
Extract from the Memorial of Captain Duncan Campbell, American Loyalist Claims.

Humbly Sheweth, that he was a native of Great Britain and he was appointed Ensign in the 42nd

Highlanders 26 January 1756, in which Corps he
served the war before last in America and the West
Indies. And in August 1763 the Regiment was ordered on an expedition to the relief of Fort Pitt, then
invested by the savages.

On the march he was severely wounded at the
battle of Bushy Run, and for a long time rendered
unfit for service. (In this skirmishing warfare the
troops suffered much from the want of water and
the extreme heat of the weather) which occasioned
his retiring on half pay in 1764.

He soon thereafter settled at Fredricksburg,
Dutchess Co. in the Prov. of New York (in 1769)
and purchased a valuable track of land from Colonel Beverly Robinson and others on good terms. In
1775 he was Colonel of Militia and Magistrate for
the said county.

That at the commencement of the troubles he
took an early and decided part in favor of His Majesty's government, which rendered him so obnoxious
to the popular party where he dwelt that he was
obliged to fly to New York, to save his life, from the
family and abandon his property in June 1775. That
soon after his arrival there he engaged as an officer
in the 2nd Battalion Highland Emigrant's in which
he continued doing duty until the cessation of hostilities, and consequent reduction of the Regiment
in Nova Scotia, in which Province he now dwells. (2
January 1784).

That early in June 1775 he got on board the *Asia*
ship of war (64 gun frigate) then stationed in New

York and soon after was joined by some recruits he had engaged to follow him. In July thereafter he went to Boston where Gen. Gage then Commander-in-Chief, gave him command of an armed transport in which he returned to New York where he enlisted and received on board about 60 more recruits. That in September he returned again to Boston where he left all his recruits except 26 which were left on board as Marines, on the 8 October he was sent back on the same service. But on the 16 of the same month was unfortunately shipwrecked on the coast of New Jersey.

On this service he lost all his money and baggage to the amount of £100. This loss His Excellency Sir William Howe, then Commander-in-Chief, would not think of reimbursing at the time.

In consequence of the shipwreck he and his party had the misfortune to be made prisoners and was carried to Philadelphia where he was fourteen months in a small apartment of the dismal goal where he contracted a sickness which was likely to prove fatal to him.

How soon he was taken his family were turned out of doors and deprived of everything they had except some wearing apparel. The distressed situation of the family so driven from their home may be easier felt than described. It brought on for a beginning the untimely death of an amiable wife, and deprived his five infant children of a mother's care whereby they for some time became objects of compassion which he was unable to rescue them from. Until he was exchanged and joined his Regiment (in January 1777) he thereafter continued to serve during the war.

Captain 4th Breadalbane Regt. of Fencibles 2nd Batt. 1 March 1793; Major 17 Feb. 1794; Lieut. Col. 9 Dec. 1795; Regiment disbanded 18 April 1799. He died at Edinburgh in Dec. 1799*.

N. B. The Memorialist was appointed Second Oldest Captain in the 2nd Batt. 84th Regiment the 14 June 1775 and was reduced in October 1783 without a step of preferment in the Regt. or in the Line.

---

* Major Sir Duncan Campbell of Barcaldin*, Bart. C.V. O. Stewart, I 279; II, Appendix No. 11.

JOHN CAMPBELL

John Campbell, of Duneaves, Perthshire, was originally a private in the Black Watch. In 1743, he was presented, with Gregor McGregor, to George II, as a specimen of the Highland soldier and performed at St. James the broadsword exercise and that of the Lochaber axe, before his Majesty and a number of General officers. Each got a gratuity of a guinea, which they gave to the porter at the gate of the palace as they passed out. Mr. Campbell obtained an Ensigncy in 1745 for his bravery at the battle of Fontenoy; was promoted to be Captain-Lieutenant, 16th February, 1756, and landed in New York the following June. He was among the few resolute men who forced their way into the work at Ticonderoga, on the 8th of July, where he was killed.

JOHN CAMPBELL

John Campbell of Glendaruel, born in 1721, was appointed Ensign of the 42nd Regt. of Foot 25th September, 1745; Lieutenant 16th May, 1748; Captain Lieut. 2nd July 1759; and Captain 20th July 1760; Captain 27th or Inniskilling Regiment of Foot 25th March 1762; Major Supt. of Indian Affairs in the Province of Quebec 2nd July, 1773; Lieut. Col. of Indian Affairs 29th August 1777; and Colonel 16th November 1790. He married Marianna St. Lucan (date not given) and died Montreal, 23rd June 1795.

In the course of a long and meritorious service with his Regiment, the 42nd Highlanders, in all its campaigns from the Rebellion in 1745 to the attack on Ticonderoga, where he was wounded on the 8th July, 1758, and the conquest of Canada, Martinique, and Havana. He subsequently served in the expedition commanded by General Burgoyne, at the head of a number of Indians, and was distinguished for his spirited conduct as an officer, adorned by that elegance and politeness which mark the accomplished gentleman and his virtues in private life endeared him to his family and companions.

His remains were attended to the grave in a manner suitable to his rank. Not only by a very numerous assembly of citizens of all ranks, but by a large body of Indian warriors, whose very decent behaviour evinced the sincerity with which they partook of the universal regret occasioned by the loss of so very respectable a member of society[*].

---

[*] Major Sir Duncan Campbell of Barcaldine, Bart. C. V. O.

JOHN CAMPBELL

John Campbell of Strachur, in the Highlands of Scotland, entered the Army in June, 1745, as Lieutenant of Loudon's Highlanders; served through the Scotch Rebellion; made the Campaign in Flanders, 1747, and was promoted to a company on the 1st October of that year. At the peace of 1748, he went on half pay and so remained until the 9th April, 1756, when he was appointed to the 42nd Highlanders previous to the embarkation of that Regiment for America. He was wounded in the attack on Ticonderoga in 1758, and was appointed by General Amherst Major of the 17th Foot on the 11th July, 1759; was promoted to be Lieutenant-Colonel in the Army, 1st February, 1762 and commanded his Regiment in the expedition that year against Martinico and Havana. On the 1st May, 1773, he became Lieutenant-Colonel of the 57th or West Middlesex Foot, returned to America in 1776 with his Regiment at the breaking out of the Revolution; was appointed Maj. General 19th February, 1779, Colonel of his Regiment 2nd November, 1780, and commanded the British Forces in West Florida, where after a gallant though ineffectual defence he was obliged to surrender Pensacola to the Spaniards 10th May, 1781. He became Lieutenant-General 28th September, 1787; General in the Army, 26th January, 1797, and died in the fore part of 1806[*].

---

[*] From Brown, IV., 155, 159. Stewart's *Sketches of the Highlanders*, I, 295, 306. 359. 370; II. 5, app. iii; Knox *Journal*, I, 373; II, 401; Beatson's *Naval and Mil. Mem.* V, 50, 226233; VI, 274-280; Army Lists. *Wilson's Orderly Book*, page 94.

MOSES CAMPBELL

A native of Scotland, joined the 42nd Regt. and was promoted Sergeant. Served with this Regiment throughout the war of French and Indians in America of 1756-63, discharged at the reduction, and settled with his family on a portion of Maj. Allan Campbell's (same Regt.) grant of land, situated on the south (bank) side of Lake Champlain, between Crown Point (about 5 miles above the point) and Ticonderoga.

Also served (possibly in the Royal Highland Emigrants, bounty 50s rendezvous Lake Champlain, 1775) in the War of Independence of 1775, (for which his property was confiscated, including boats.)

He died in active (British) service on the 18th Feb. 1781. His widow, Elizabeth, and seven children claimed 366 pounds for losses, allowed 80 pounds.

N. B. On behalf of her son, Alexander, (aged 21 years), 50 pounds, who complained that one of the rebels was now living in his house, Feb. 1783.

GORDON GRAHAM

Gordon Graham of Drainie in the Highlands of Scotland, was appointed ensign in the 43rd Highlanders in October 25, 1739, and was made lieutenant June 24, 1743. He served in Flanders and shared in the defeat at Fontenoy in 1745, after which the Regiment returned home. In 1747 he made another campaign in Flanders. On August 7, 1747, he was appointed captain. In 1749 the number of the regiment was changed to the 42nd and Mr. Graham obtained a company in it 3rd June,

1752, came to America in 1756, was at the surrender of Fort William Henry under Colonel Munro in 1757, and was wounded at Ticonderoga in 1758. The Major of the Regiment having been killed on that occasion Captain Graham succeeded to the vacancy, July 17th, 1758, and made the campaign of 1759 and 1760 under Amherst. He next served in the West Indies in the expedition against Martinique and July 9, 1762, became Lieutenant Colonel of the Regiment, which returned to New York, and in the year 1763, proceeded to the relief of Fort Pitt, defeating the Indians on the way in the Battle of Bushy Run. In December, 1770, he retired after 31 years of service in the Regiment. As his name does not appear in the army list of 1771 it is presumed that he died at this time[*].

[*] From Brown's *Highland Clans* IV, 139, 159. Beatson's *Naval and Mil. Mem.* II, 530. Wilson's *Orderly Book*, p. 14.

JOHN GRAHAM

John Graham was the brother of Thomas; entered the 42nd regiment as Ensign and was promoted to a Lieutenancy 25th January, 1776; was wounded at Ticonderoga 1758; became Captain in February, 1762, and was again wounded at Bushy Run in 1763; shortly after which his company having been disbanded, he went on half pay. He rejoined the regiment 25th December, 1765, and is dropped in 1772, having attained the rank of field officer[*].

[*] From Stewart I, 359, Army Lists. *N.Y. Col. Manuscripts*, p. 729, Vol. 10.

THOMAS GRAHAM

Thomas Graham, or Graeme, of Duchay, entered the 43rd, or Black Watch, as Ensign June 30, 1741; was promoted to a Lieutenancy August 6, 1746, and obtained a company February 15, 1756, shortly before the regiment, then the 42nd, came to America. He served in the several Campaigns on the northern lakes; was wounded at Ticonderoga in 1758; was again wounded at the battle of Bushy Run, near Pittsburgh, in 1763; served in the subsequent campaigns against the Indians, and embarked for Ireland in 1767. He succeeded Major Reid 31st March, 1770, and became Lieutenant-Colonel 12th December following. He retired from the army December, 1771, after 30 years of service[*].

Army Lists. Stewart. *N.Y. Colonial Manuscripts*, p. 729, Vol. 10.

FRANCIS GRANT

Francis Grant, son of the Laird of Grant, and brother of Sir Ludovick Grant, of Grant, Scotland, was received from half pay in Loudon's Regiment and was made ensign in the Black Watch October 25th, 1739. November 5th, 1739, he was made lieutenant; June 18th, 1743, captain; and October 3rd, 1745, he became major. A vacancy occurring in the lieutenant-colonelcy, in December, 1755, the men of the Regiment subscribed a sum of money among themselves to purchase the step for him, but it was not required; he had already obtained his promotion. He accompanied the Regiment to America in 1756 and was present at the bloody battle of Ticonderoga, July 8th, 1758, where he was wounded. In the following year he accompanied Amherst on his expedition, and in 1760 was in command of the van of the Army from Oswego to Montreal. In 1761 he commanded the Army sent to the south to chastise the Cherokees. He served as Brigadier-General in the expedition against Martinico in 1762, and on the 19th of February of that year became colonel in the army. On July 9th, 1762, after twenty-three years of service in the Black Watch Regiment, he was removed and appointed to the command of the 90th Light Infantry. In August, 1762, he commanded the 4th Brigade at the siege of Havana and went on half pay at the peace of 1763. In November, 1768, he became colonel of the 63rd; Major-General in 1770; and Lieutenant-General in 1777. He died at the beginning of 1782 Lieut.-Gen. Grant's daughter was married to the Hon. and Rt. Rev. George Murray, fourth son of the Duke of Athol, and Bishop of St. David's*.

---

* From *Brown's Highland Clans*, IV, 155. Knox's *Journal*, II, 404, 410, 465. Beatson *N. and M., Mem.* Ill, 363, 359. *Debrett's Peerage.* Wilson's *Orderly Book*, p. 3.

JAMES GRANT

James Grant, appointed Ensign, November 20th, 1746; Lieutenant, Jan. 22nd, 1756; Captain, Dec. 26th, 1760; removed Aug. 13th, 1762, after 16 years of service in the Regiment and was made Fort-Major Limerick. Died in 1778. He was wounded at Ticonderoga*.

---

* From Stewart of Garth, Appendix.

WILLIAM GRANT

William Grant, appointed Ensign, October 1st, 1745; Lieutenant, May 22nd, 1746; Captain, July 23rd, 1758; Major, Dec. 5th, 1777; retired August, 1778, after 33 years of service with rank of Brevet Lieut.-Colonel. He was wounded at the battle of Ticonderoga*.

* From Stewart of Garth, Appendix.

JAMES GRAY

James Gray was taken from the half pay list and appointed Lieutenant in the 42nd Royal Highlanders 30th January, 1756. His name is omitted in the Army List of 1765*.

* From Stewart's Highlanders. Wilson's *Orderly Book*, page 83.

ROBERT GRAY

Robert Gray, appointed Ensign, June 6th, 1745; Lieutenant, June 9th, 1747; Captain, July 22nd, 1758. He was wounded at Ticonderoga. Aug. 2nd, 1759, after 14 years of service in the Regiment, he was promoted to the 55th Regiment. He died in 1771 with rank of Lieut.-Colonel*.

* From Stewart of Garth, Appendix.

ALEXANDER MCINTOSH

Alexander McIntosh was taken from half pay in 1756 and appointed Lieutenant in the 42nd. He was wounded at Ticonderoga, 1758, and again at Martinico in 1762, and was promoted to a company 24th July of the same year. He went on half pay in 1763 and was not again called on active service until 25th December, 1770, when he was appointed to the 10th regiment then serving in America. Captain McIntosh was killed at the storming of Fort Washington, 16th November, 1776*.

* Army Lists. Beateon's *Naval and Military Memoirs*. *N.Y. Colonial Manuscripts*, p. 729. Vol. 10.

NORMAN McLEOD

Norman McLeod entered the army as ensign of the 42nd January 1756, and was promoted to Lieutenancy in the 69th in June 1761. At the peace of 1763 he elected to remain in this country and received 3,000 acres of land and retired on half pay. Sometime later he was appointed Commissioner at Niagara under Sir William Johnson. At the breaking out of the War of the Revolution he offered his services to Governor Martin of North Carolina. Later he was captured and was a prisoner for about five years*.

* Wm. M. McBean, Secy. St. Andrew's Society of the State of New York.

JOHN MACNEIL

John MacNeil was appointed ensign, Aug. 6th, 1742, lieutenant October 10th, 1745; Captain, Dec. 16th, 1752; Major, July 9th, 1762. He died at the siege of Havana in 1762 after 20 years of service in the Regiment*.

* From Stewart of Garth, Appendix.

DAVID MILNE

David Mill, or Milne, received a commission as Lieutenant in this Corps 19th July, 1757; was wounded at

Ticonderoga in 1758, and again at Martinique in 1762; retired from the army at the peace of 1763*.

---

* From *N.Y. Colonial Manuscripts*, p. 729, Vol. 10.

JAMES MURRAY

James Murray, second son of Lord George Murray, by his marriage with Amelia Murray, heiress of Strowan and Glencaree, and grandson of the first Duke of Atholl, was born at Tullibardine on the 19th of March, 1734, and it is interesting to know that Lord John Murray, who was destined in after years to be his colonel, was called upon to be his godfather. A commission as Lieutenant in the Saxon Grenadier Guards was obtained for him in 1749, and he joined his regiment in 1751. He served against the forces of Frederick the Great until the Saxon Army capitulated at Pirna on the Elbe in October, 1756. He was released on parole and returned to Scotland in 1757 and on the nomination of his uncle, James Duke of Atholl, was given a captain's commission in the Black Watch and was placed in command of one of the three additional companies then being raised for service in America. He reached New York in April, 1758, and commanded Captain Reid's company in the unsuccessful attack on Ticonderoga, his own company having been left in garrison at Fort Edward. He was wounded but was soon able to return to duty and took part in the successful expedition of 1759 to Lake Champlain. Toward the close of that year he was given command by Lord John Murray's desire of the Grenadier Company of the newly-raised 2nd Battalion, and with this battalion he served in the advance on Montreal in 1760 and in the capture of Martinique in 1762. He was wounded here and invalided home and was on sick leave for more than six years.* He rejoined the Black Watch in 1768 and in 1769 was appointed Captain-Lieutenant in the 3rd Foot Guards, obtaining his promotion as Captain and Lieutenant-Colonel the following year. In 1772 he was elected member of Parliament for Perthshire, a position which he held for twenty-two years. He was appointed Governor of Upnor Castle in 1775 and Fort William in 1780, but these were merely nominal posts and did not interfere with his other duties. In 1776 he bought Strowan (originally the property of his mother), from his nephew, the fourth Duke of Atholl.

On the outbreak of the War of Independence, Col. Murray offered to raise a regiment of Highlanders for service in America, but this offer was refused, and in March, 1777, he was sent out to join the brigade of Guards under General Howe in New Jersey. He was with Lord Cornwallis at Quibbletown and presumably took part in the actions at Brandywine and Germantown in 1777. He spent the following winter in quarters at Philadelphia, and left America in the summer of 1778 and joined the Atholl Highlanders in Ireland in September of that year, of which regiment he was given the command. This regiment remained in Ireland during the war, at the conclusion of which it was disbanded. James Murray was appointed Lieutenant-Colonel-Commandant of the 78th Highlanders in 1783, but as he was already a general officer he never did any duty with this regiment. After 1783 General Murray resided a good deal at Strowan; in

1786 he was promoted full Colonel of the 78th (by that time the 72nd), and in 1793 he was made Lieutenant-General. In March, 1794, he felt himself obliged to resign his seat in Parliament owing to ill health and a few days later on the 19th of March he died in London and was buried in St. Margaret's, Westminster.

Of Lord George Murray's three sons, General James seems to have been the one who most resembled his father. He had inherited the Jacobite General's sympathetic knowledge of Highland character, something of his pride, and the same affectionate disposition. And that he had at least a share of his father's determination, and presence of mind is shown by two anecdotes which have been handed down with regard to him. One of these refers to his earlier days, and is to the effect that, having been attacked by a highwayman one night that he was driving over a heath near London, he leant out of the window of the chaise, "groped in the dark for the ears of his assailant's horse," and with the brief but expressive exclamation "Thereut's—" fired a shot which ended the highwayman's career. The other relates that during the Gordon Riots of 1780 Colonel James Murray was seated next Lord George Gordon in the House of Commons at the very moment at which the mob threatened to break into the House. Colonel Murray with a soldier's instinct drew his sword, pointed it at Lord George, and notwithstanding that he was his cousin, declared his intention of running him through the body if a single one of the rioters should enter. His promptness saved the situation, but he had committed a breach of the privileges of the House and was ordered to apologise on bended knee to the Speaker. Colonel Murray made the required *amende*, but on rising from his knee took out his handkerchief and dusted it, remarking: "Damned Dirty House this; sooner it's cleaned out the better."[**]

---

[*] Stewart of Garth gives the following: in regard to General Murray's wound, received at the capture of Martinique (page 126, Vol. 10.):

The musket ball entered his left side, under the lower rib, Passed up through the left lobe of the lung, (as ascertained after his death) crossed his chest, and mounting up to his right shoulder, lodged under the scapula. His case being considered desperate, the only object of the surgeon was to make his situation as easy as possible for the few hours they supposed he had to live; but, to the great surprise of all, he was on .his legs in a few weeks, and, before he reached England, was quite recovered, or at least his health and appetite were restored. He was afterwards however, able to lie down; and during the thirty-two years of his subsequent life, he slept in an upright posture, supported in his bed by pillows.

[**] Army Lists: Brown's *Highl. Clans*, IV, 159, 300, 304, 306. Wilson's *Orderly Book*, p. 67. *Military History of Perthshire*, p. 411-413.

LORD JOHN MURRAY

Lord John Murray, born on the 14th of April, 1711, was the eldest son of John, first Duke of Atholl, by his second wife, the Hon. Mary Ross, and half-brother to John, Marquess of Tullibardine, and Lord George Murray. He became an ensign in the 3rd Foot Guards (now the Scots Guards) in 1727, and a captain in the same regiment in 1738. Immediately after the mutiny of the regiment in 1743 he applied for the colonelcy in the 42nd or Black Watch, but he did not obtain the appointment he so greatly desired until two years later. In July, 1743, he was appointed first aide-de-camp to George II and was in attendance on the King in Germany at the close of the Dettingen campaign, but returned to England without having taken part in any engagements. In April 1745, when at last gazetted colonel of the Black Watch, he proceeded to join his regiment in Flanders, but arrived too late for Fontenoy. He distinguished himself, however, during the subsequent retreat of the British army to Brussels, by his defence of a pass which the French attacked by night. For this service he was publicly thanked by the Duke of Cumberland. In 1745 he returned home with his regiment but in 1747 he was in the Netherlands taking part in the attempted relief of Hulst. After the surrender of the town by the Dutch Governor, Lord John commanded the rearguard in the retreat to Welsharden, and shortly afterwards, having been ordered to take part in the defence of Bergen-op-Zoom, he was placed in command of the British troops in the lines there. At the close of operations he received a message of approbation from the King.

In 1755 he was promoted Major-General, and in 1758 Lieutenant-General, but although he offered his services more than once, he was not employed abroad during the Seven Years' War. He took the keenest interest, however, in all the exploits of his regiment and worked hard to raise a second battalion in 1758. Stewart of Garth tells us that when the men who had been disabled at Ticonderoga appeared before the Board of Chelsea to claim their pensions, Lord John went with them and explained their case in such a manner to the commissioners that they were all successful. He gave them money, got them a free passage to Perth, and offered a house and garden to all who chose to settle on his estate. General Stewart also describes how, when the 42nd at last returned from America in 1767, Lord John, who had been for weeks at Cork awaiting its arrival, marched into that town at its head.

Lord John was a great deal with the regiment while it was quartered in Ireland, and, according to Stewart of Garth, was "ever attentive to the interest of the officers and vigilant that their promotion should not be interrupted by ministerial or other influence." He was also "unremitting in his exertions to procure the appointment of good officers, and of officers who understood perfectly the peculiar dispositions and character of the men." For this reason he strenuously endeavoured to exclude all but the members of Scots and more especially Highland families. He was equally particular that only Gaelic-speaking men and Protestants should be recruited for the ranks.

In spite of his military duties Lord John resided a good deal in the country and not only at the home of his boyhood for early in life he bought Pitnacree in Strathtay, and in later years he had also a house in Perth. He represented Perthshire in Parliament from 1734 to 1761. In 1758 he married Miss Dalton of Bannercross a Derbyshire heiress, by whom he had one daughter. In 1770 he became a full general. His last military achievement was the raising in 1779 and 1780 (at his own expense) of another second battalion to the 42nd. This battalion so distinguished itself in India that in 1786 it was placed permanently on the establishment under the title of the 73rd Regiment, the veteran to whose patriotism it owed its existence died on the 26th day of May, 1787, at the age of seventy-six, the senior officer in the Army.

Lord John made the most of such chances as occurred of distinguishing himself in the field, but those opportunities were small for he never served in any war but the Austrian Succession.

It is therefore as the Colonel of the Black Watch that his name has survived as a man who understood the Highland soldiers well enough to wish to command them at a time when to many that might have seemed a task of great difficulty and who, having at last obtained the post he desired, completely identified himself with the interests of his men, and for upwards of half a century was the "friend and supporter of every deserving officer and soldier in the regiment*.

---

* From *Military History of Perthshire.*

JOHN REID

John Reid was the eldest son of Alexander Robertson of Straloch, but the head of the family had always been known as "Baron Reid" and the General and his younger brother, Alexander (who was an officer in the 42nd), adopted the more distinctive surname early in life. He was born at Inverchroskie in Strathardle, on the 13th of February, 1721, and received his early education at Perth. Being destined for the law, he was afterwards sent to Edinburgh University. Nature, however, had intended him for a soldier, and in June, 1745, having recruited the necessary quota of men, he obtained a commission as lieutenant in Loudon's Highlanders. He was taken prisoner at Preston-pans the following September, but when released the following spring he rejoined his regiment and was able to render important service to the Government. From 1747 to 1748 he served in Flanders with Loudon's Highlanders and took part in the defence of Bergen-op-Zoom, but on the reduction of his regiment at the Peace of Aix-la-Chapelle he was placed on half-pay. In 1751 he bought a captain-lieutenant's commission in the Black Watch and in 1752 a commission as captain in the same regiment. Four years later on the outbreak of the war with France, he sailed with his regiment to America. He was not present at the first attack on Ticonderoga as he had been left behind sick at Albany, and his company was commanded in that desperate engagement by Captain James Murray. In 1759, Reid, by that time a major, took part in the second advance to Lake Champlain, which resulted in the surrender of Forts Ticonderoga and Crown Point; and on him devolved the command of the 42nd during the greater part of the campaign of 1760 which ended with the capture of Montreal and the expulsion of the French from Canada.

Reid remained in America with the 42nd until Dec., 1761, when he accompanied it to the West Indies. He served in the capture of Martinique and at the storming of Morne Tortenson, on Jan. 24, 1762, was in command of the 1st Battalion of his regiment. His battalion suffered heavy loss and he was wounded in two places, but recovered in time to take part in the expedition against Havana of that same year. After the surrender of Cuba he returned to America. In 1764 Reid acted as second-in-command of Colonel Bouquet's arduous but successful expedition against the Indians on the Ohio and Muskingum Rivers.

In the following year we hear of him fitting out an expedition which was to be sent to the Illinois country under the command of Captain Thomas Stirling of the 42nd.

About 1760, Reid married an American lady of Scots descent, Susanna Alexander, daughter of James Alexander, surveyor-general of New York and New Jersey. She owned property on Otter Creek in what is now the State of Vermont, which was added to and improved by her husband with the result that at the end of ten years Reid owned "about thirty-five thousand acres of very valuable land" near Crown Point and had "obtained from the Governor and Council of New York a warrant of survey for fifteen thousand more," which he intended to "erect" into a manor.

In 1767 the Royal Highland Regiment left America for Ireland and Reid presumably accompanied it. In 1770 Reid retired on half -pay, intending no doubt to settle down to the enjoyment and improvement of his American estates. However, in 1772 his tenants were expelled by the people of Bennington "on the pretence of having claim to that country under the Government of New Hampshire, notwithstanding that the King in Council had, ten years before, decreed Connecticut River to be the Eastern Boundary of New York." In 1775 war broke out with the American colonists, and though his case finally came before the Commissioners for American Claims, the only compensation awarded him was a trifling allowance for mills he had erected and for fees he had paid for surveys. In May, 1778 his father's estate, Straloch, passed under the hammer as he was unable to pay the mortgages and his son could give him no help.

Notwithstanding that he was a comparatively poor

man, in 1779-1780 Reid raised at his own expense a regiment of foot, of which he was appointed colonel. This was called the 95th and was disbanded in 1783. In 1781 Reid was promoted major-general, and in 1793 a lieutenant-general. He was appointed colonel of the 88th Regiment (Connaught Rangers) in November, 1794, and became a general in 1798. In 1803, when an invasion was hourly expected, Reid, in response to an order that all general officers not employed on the staff should transmit their addresses to the Adjutant-General, wrote that though in the eighty-second years of his age "and very deaf and infirm," he was still ready to use his feeble arm in defence of his country. He died in the Haymarket on the 6th of February, 1807, and was buried in St. Margaret's, Westminster.

The General would probably have had but little property to dispose of at his death, had he not in 1796 succeeded to a valuable estate of some four or five thousand acres in Nova Scotia, which was left to him by his cousin, Gen. John Small, "as a mark of .... respect .... and attachment to the preservation of his name and representation for succeeding ages." Reid's daughter had made a marriage of which he disapproved, she had no children, and his only brother had died in 1762 during the siege of Havana. It was probably these circumstances that induced him to realize the property in Nova Scotia and at the time of his death he was worth some 52,000. This entire fortune, went after the death of his daughter, to the University of Edinburgh to found a musical professorship. He also left directions that a concert should be given annually on or about his birthday to commence with several pieces of his own composition, among the first of which is that of the *Garb of Old Gaul*, a composition written by Sir Charles Erskine, but set to music by Reid while major of the 42nd, and which has ever since been a regimental march.

Reid also composed several military marches and was esteemed the best gentleman player on the German flute in England. It may safely be predicted that as long as the University exists this old Perthshire soldier of the 18th century will be remembered as one of its benefactors*.

---

* *N.Y. Documentary History* IV. *Military History of Perthshire.*

JOHN SMALL.

John Small was the third son of Patrick Small, who married Magdalen Robertson, sister of Alexander Robertson, the father of General John Reid. Reid and Small were thus not only neighbours and brother-officers, but first cousins, and were evidently on terms of close friendship. Born in Strathardle, Atholl, Scotland, in 1730, Small, like many of his countrymen of that date, began his military career with the Scots Brigade in Holland, being appointed a 2nd lieutenant in the Earl of Drumlanrig's Regiment when it was raised for service of the States-General in 1747. How long he remained abroad is unknown but it is probable that he returned to England when the regiment was reduced in 1752. He did not, however, obtain a commission in the British army until four years later, when he was appointed lieutenant in the 42nd, just prior to its departure for America. So far as is known, Small took part in all the campaigns in which his regiment was engaged from 1756 to 1763. He fought at Ticonderoga in 1758, served with General Amherst's successful expedition to Lake Champlain in the following year, and took part in the operations which completed the conquest of Canada in 1760. After the surrender of Montreal he was sent in charge of French prisoners to New York, and we learn from a brother officer that General Amherst had great confidence in him, and frequently employed him "on particular services." Two years later he served in the capture of Martinique and Havana and obtained his promotion as captain.

At the peace of 1763 Small was placed on half-pay, but, according to General Stewart, he was almost immediately put on the full-pay list of the North British Fusiliers (21st) and when in 1767 the Black Watch left for Europe, most of the men of that regiment who had volunteered to stay in America joined the Fusiliers in order to serve under Small, who was "deservedly popular" with them. Small, however, cannot have served long with the 21st, for in the same year in which the Black Watch left America he was appointed "major of brigade" to the forces in North America.

It was probably during the interval between the Seven Years' War and the war with the Americans that he began to acquire the property in Nova Scotia, part of which he afterwards bequeathed to his cousin, John Reid. We have some indication that during this period he interested himself in local politics and formed the friendship of at least one American which was of value to him later.

Small served throughout the War of Independence though but rare glimpses are obtained of him. He was present as a Brigade Major at the battle of Bunker Hill, June 17, 1777, and in the course of that day his life was saved by the American General Putnam, who, seeing Small standing alone at a time when all around him had fallen, struck up the barrels of his men's muskets to save his life. Shortly after this, Small raised the 2nd battalion of the Royal Highland Regiment and was appointed major-commandant. In 1778 the regiment was numbered the 84th and in 1780 he was promoted to Lieutenant-Colonel-Commandant of his battalion. He is said to have joined Sir Henry Clinton at New York in 1779, but it is more probable that he was stationed for the most part in Nova Scotia. In March, 1783, Small and his battalion were at Fort Edward, New York, and in the following autumn the battalion was disbanded at Windsor, Nova Scotia, where many of the men settled and formed the present town of Douglas.

Small, once more on half pay, returned home and in 1790 was promoted colonel and three years later was appointed lieutenant governor of Guernsey. In October, 1794, he became Major-General and on the 17th of March, 1796, he died in Guernsey and was buried in the church of St. Peter Port.

General Stewart of Garth wrote of General John Small that "No chief of former days ever more fairly secured the attachment of his clan, and no chief, certainly, ever deserved it better. With an enthusiastic and almost romantic love for his country and countrymen, it seemed as if the principal object of his life had been to serve them, and promote prosperity. Equally brave in leading them in the field, and kind, just, and conciliating in quarters, they would have indeed been ungrateful if they regarded him otherwise than as they did. There was not an instance of desertion in his battalion."*

* Stewart II. 143. *Military Hist., of Perthshire*, pp. 396-399.

JAMES STEWART

James Stewart of Urrard, obtained a company in the 42nd, July 18th, 1757. He was wounded at Ticonderoga, 1758. He sold out after the peace*.

* Stewart I, 306, 359. *N.Y. Col. MSS.*, p. 729, Vol. 10.

THOMAS STIRLING

Thomas Stirling, second son of Sir Henry Stirling, of Ardoch, was born October 8, 1731. He began his military career in the Dutch service, being given a commission as Ensign in the 1st Battalion of Col. Marjoribanks' Regiment on the 30th of September, 1747, and was probably placed on half-pay when the establishment of the Scots Brigade was reduced in 1752. On the 24th of July, 1757, having been nominated by James, Duke of Atholl, and having raised the requisite number of men, he was gazetted captain of one of the three companies added to the 42nd in that year. In November, 1757, he sailed for America, where he served with his regiment in the campaigns of the ensuing years, though he was not present at the first attack on Ticonderoga, owing to the fact that the new companies had been left behind to garrison Fort Edward. He took part in the capture of Martinique in 1762 and was wounded but was able to serve in the capture of Havana later in that year. He returned with his regiment to America and in August, 1765, was sent in command of a company to take possession of Fort de Chartes on the Mississippi. After holding this fort that winter and spring, he returned with his detachment to the regiment in June, 1766. The following year the 42nd left America and for upwards of eight years was quartered in Ireland, after which it was for a short time" in Scotland. In 1770 Stirling was gazetted Major of the regiment, and 1771 Lieutenant-Colonel-Commandant. Hostilities broke out with the Americans in 1775, and, Stirling, having in five months raised the strength of his regiment from 350 men to 1,200, returned with it in the following spring to America, where he commanded it continuously for three years during the war. He took part in the engagement at Brooklyn, the attack on Fort Washington, the expedition to Pennsylvania, battle of Monmouth, and others. During 1778-9 he was stationed at or near New York. In June, 1779, he accompanied a force under General Mathews through New Jersey in an attempt to rally the supposed loyalists of that state. This was unsuccessful and ended in the destruction of the town of Springfield. General Stirling was so severely wounded while leading the attack that he could take no further part in the war. His thigh was broken and fearing to be rendered incapable of further service he refused to have it amputated. He recovered and was invalided home but he does not appear after this to have been ever again fit for active duty. In 1782 he was promoted Major-General and appointed Colonel of the 71st Foot, but his regiment was disbanded the following year. His services were rewarded with a baronetcy and in 1790, he became colonel of the 41st Regiment. In 1796 he was promoted Lieutenant-General, and in 1799 he succeeded his brother in the baronetcy of Ardock. He attained the rank of General in 1801 and died unmarried on the 9th of May, 1808.

KENNETH TOLMIE

Kenneth Tolmie was commissioned a ieutenant in the 42nd Highlanders, 23rd January, 1756, and promoted to the Command of a Company 27th July, 1760. His name is dropped after the Peace of 1763*.

---

* Wilson's *Orderly Book*, p. 166.

ALEXANDER TURNBULL

Alexander Turnbull of Stracathro, appointed Ensign, June 3, 1752; ieutenant, September 27, 1756; Captain, Aug. 14, 1762. After 11 years of service, he went on half pay in 1763; full pay of the 32nd Foot. He died in 1804 with rank of Major*.

---

* Stewart of Garth, Appendix.

Original Regimental List of the Black Watch

FROM A MILITARY HISTORY OF PERTHSHIRE, AND THE BLACK WATCH CHRONICLE

No. 1 COMPANY

Colonel and Captain John, Earl of Crawford. Died 1748.

Captain-Lieutenant Duncan Mackfarland. Retired 1744.

Ensign Gilbert Stewart of Kincraigie.

No. 2 COMPANY

Lieutenant-Colonel and Captain Sir Robert Munro, Bart., of Foulis. Killed at Falkirk 1746. Lieutenant Paul MacPherson.

Ensign Archibald Macnab, younger son of the Laird of Macnab. Died Lieut. General, 1790.

No. 3 COMPANY

Major and Captain George Grant. Removed from the service by sentence of Court-martial, 1746.

Lieutenant John MacKenzie of Rencraig (?Kincraig).

Ensign Collin Campbell.

No. 4 COMPANY

Captain Collin Campbell, Jr., of Monzie. Retired 1743.

Lieutenant Alexander Macdonald

Ensign James Campbell of Glenfalloch. Died of

wounds at Fontenoy.

No. 5 Company

Captain James Colquhoun of Luss. Promoted to be Major. Retired in 1748.

Lieutenant George Ramsay.

Ensign James Campbell of Stronslanie.

No. 6 Company

Captain John Campbell of Carrick. Killed at Fontenoy.

Lieutenant John MacLean of Kingairloch.

Ensign Dougall Stewart (of Appin?).

No. 7 Company

Captain Collin Campbell of Balliemore. Retired.

Lieutenant Malcom Frazer, son of Culduthel.1 Killed at Bergen-op-Zoom, 1747.

Ensign Dougal Stewart.

No. 8 Company

Captain George Munro of Culcairn, brother of Foulis. Killed 1746.

Lieutenant Lewis Grant of Auchterblair.

Ensign John Menzies of Comrie.

No. 9 Company

Captain Dougal Campbell of Craignish. Retired in 1745.

Lieutenant John Mackneil.

Ensign Gordon Graham of Draines.

No. 10 Company

Captain John Monro of Newmore. Promoted to be Lt. Col. 1743; retired 1749.

Lieutenant Francis Grant, son of the Laird of Grant. Died Lieut.-General 1782.

Ensign Edward Carrick.

Surgeon George Monro.

Quarter Master John Forbes.

Chaplain Hon. Gideon Murray.

Adjutant John Lindsay.

APPENDIX M

Officers of the
42nd Royal Highland Regiment

FROM THE BRITISH ARMY LIST
20TH JUNE, 1759.

Col. Lord Jno. Murray, Lt. Gen.

Lt. Col. Francis Grant

Major Gordon Graham

Capt. James Abercrombie

Capt. Allan Campbell

Capt. Archibald Campbell

Capt. John Campbell

Capt. Thomas Graeme

Capt. William Grant

Capt. David Haldane

Capt. Francis McLean

Capt. John McNeil

Capt. James Murray

Capt. William Murray

Capt. Alexander Reid

Capt. John Reid

Capt. James Stewart

Capt. Alexander St. Clair

Capt. Thomas Stirling

Capt. John Stuart

Capt. Lieut. Robert Gray

Lieut. Patrick Balneavis

Lieut. Simon Blair

Lieut. David Barclay

Lieut. Alex. Campbell

Lieut. Arch. Campbell

Lieut. Archibald Campbell

Lieut. Donald Campbell

Lieut. Duncan Campbell

Lieut. James Campbell

Lieut. John Campbell, Sen.

Lieut. John Campbell

Lieut. John Campbell, Jr

Lieut. Gordon Clunes

Lieut. Alex. Farquharson

Lieut. James Fraser

Lieut. John Graham

Lieut. George Grant

Lieut. James Grant

Lieut. John Grant

Lieut. Peter Grant

Lieut. James Gray

Lieut. Archibald Lament

Lieut. George Leslie

Lieut. Alex Mackay

Lieut. Alex. McIntosh

Lieut. James McIntosh

Lieut. Alex. McLean

Lieut. Robert Menzies

Lieut. David Mills

Lieut. John Murray

Lieut. John Robertson

Lieut. Robert Robertson

Lieut. George Sinclair

Lieut. George Sinclair

Lieut. John Small

Lieut. John Smith

Lieut. Adam Stuart

Lieut. Kenneth Tolme

Lieut. Alex. Turnbull

Ensign William Brown

Ensign Archibald Campbell

Ensign Archibald Campbell

Ensign Thomas Cunison

Ensign Alex. Donaldson

Ensign Thomas Fletcher

Ensign John Gordon

Ensign John Graham

Ensign Allen Grant

Ensign Lewis Grant

Ensign John Gregor

Ensign Elbert Herring

Ensign John Leith

Ensign William McIntosh

Ensign Neil McLean

Ensign Archibald McNab

Ensign Charles Menzies

Ensign Patrick Sinclair

Ensign John Chas. St. Clair

Sergt. Phineas McPherson

Chaplain James Stewart

Adj. James Grant.

Aldj. Alex McLean

Quarter Master John Graham

Quarter Master Adam Stewart

Surgeon Robt. Drummond

Surgeon David Hepburn

Agt., Mr. Drummond, Spring Garden.

The following corrections were interlined in ink in the above Army List of 1759, which was found in the British Museum:

Capt. John Reid was made Major. Aug. 5, 1759.

Capt. John Campbell, removed to the 17th.

Capt. David Haldane, removed to a Regiment at Jamaica.

Lieut. Alexander McLean, made captain of corps of Highlanders.

Lieut. George Sinclair, dead.

Lieut. George Sinclair, removed to Crawford's Regiment.

Ensign Thomas Fletcher, made lieutenant June 1, 1759.

Ensign William McIntosh, removed to Keith's Corps.

Sergt. Phineas McPherson, made ensign June 1, 1759.

Lauchlan Johnson, made chaplain 20th August, 1759, in place of James Stewart.

Alexander Donaldson, made adjutant 20th March, 1759, in place of Alexander McLean.

The Black Watch in the 1759 Campaign

FROM COMMISSARY WILSON'S ORDERLY BOOK

ALBANY, 22ND MAY, 1759

Two companies of the Royal Highland Regiment are also to receive *batteaux* and load them with provision and baggage. A sergeant and 12 men of the Rhode Island Regiment are to relieve a party of the Royal Highland Regiment at the Half Way House on the way to Schenectady; they are to march tomorrow morning and carry six days' provision with them.

ALBANY, 23RD MAY, 1759

Three captains of the Royal Highlanders summoned among others to a general Court Martial, of which Col. Francis Grant was President, to set tomorrow at the Town House in

Albany at 3 o'clock to try all prisoners that may be brought before them.

Albany, 26th May, 1759

An officer and 25 men of the Royal Highland Regiment with a week's provision to be sent this afternoon to Widow McGinnes House to protect settlement; one Company of the Royal Highland Regiment to march tomorrow morning at 5 o'clock; they will take their tents and camp equipage with them, for which a wagon will be allowed on sending to Col. Bradstreet for it; the officer commanding that company to call upon the General this night. The General Court Martial of which Col. Grant is President to meet again tomorrow at 8 o'clock.

Albany, 31st May, 1759

The Royal Highland Regiment to march tomorrow morning at 5 o'clock to Halfmoon, where they will take the artillery under their charge and escort the same to Fort Edward.

Fort Edward, 6th June, 1759

Lieut. Col. Robinson will mark out the Camp tomorrow morning at 5 o'clock that the Regiments may take up their ground as they arrive; the Regiments to encamp. . . . Royal

Highlanders on the right. A Sergeant and 16 men of the Royal Highlanders to take the General's Guard.

FORT EDWARD, 7TH JUNE, 1759

The Regiments are not to change their encampment until the ground be quite dry.

FORT EDWARD, 8TH JUNE, 1759

The Regiments to change their encampment this day at 12 o'clock.

FORT EDWARD, 9TH JUNE, 1759

Field Officer for the piquet tomorrow, Major Graham. The Light infantry of the Highland Regiment is to practice firing ball tomorrow morning at 6 o'clock, near the Royal Block House on the other side of the river.

The Royal Highland Regiment to furnish 2 captains, 6 subs., and 200 men. . . .; this detachment to take *batteaux* tomorrow morning at day break. The Royal Highland Regiment to take 20 *batteaux*, and 60 of the 200 men with arms to serve as a covering party. The whole to take provisions for tomorrow with them; they are to proceed to Col. Haviland's Camp, opposite to Fort Miller, where the commanding officer will apply to Col. Haviland who will order the *batteaux* to be immediately loaded,

that the whole party may return to Fort
Edward without loss of time.

FORT EDWARD, 10TH JUNE, 1759

Field Officer for the piquet this night Major (Gordon)
Graham, for tomorrow Major (Allen) Campbell,
Colonel of the day, Col. (Francis) Grant. Two
captains of the Royal Highlanders to sit with
others in General Court Martial tomorrow
morning at 8 o'clock, to try such prisoners as are
on the Provost Guard. The Royal Highlanders
and Montgomery's Regiments to send as many
men this afternoon at 4 o'clock as are necessary
to clean the ground where the Light Infantry is
to encamp. They will receive axes on applying
to the store-keeper in the Fort, which they will
return when they have finished that work.

FORT EDWARD, 11TH JUNE, 1759

Colonel of the day, Col. Grant, Field Officer of the
piquets, Major Campbell.

FORT EDWARD, 12TH JUNE, 1759

Block Houses to be relieved tomorrow by the Line
. . . . the one joining the east side of the Bridge
by 1 Sub., 2 Sergeants, 2 corpls. and 24 men of
the Royal Highlanders; the one in the front of
the Right of the Royal, one Sergeant, one Corpl.
and 10 men of the Royal Highlanders.

FORT EDWARD, 13TH JUNE, 1759

The Royal Highland Regiment to strike their tents tomorrow at Reveille Beating. The Royal Highlanders posted in their Block Houses as per ordered of yesterday, to be relieved immediately.

FORT EDWARD, 17TH JUNE, 1759

The First Battalion Massachusetts to strike their tents at Reveille Beating and march half an hour after to the Halfway Brook where the commanding officer will put himself under the command of Col. Grant.

FORT EDWARD, 19TH JUNE, 1759

The Royal Highlanders will furnish one Sub. and 30 men towards the working party required tomorrow to repair the roads.

FORT EDWARD, 20TH JUNE 1759

Capt. Campbell of the Royal Highland Grenediers is appointed Major to the Battalion of Grenediers for the Campaign.

LAKE GEORGE, 22ND JUNE, 1759

The Royal Highlanders to receive one day's fresh beef tomorrow.

Lake George 24th June, 1759

Field Officer for tomorrow, Major Graham.

Lake George, 26th June, 1759

The Royal Highlanders to receive 7 days' provisions tomorrow.

Lake George, 27th June, 1759

Generals Guard tomorrow, Royal Highlanders. 2 Companies of Grenediers with 2 Companies of Light Infantry ordered this morning with as many Rangers and Indians as Maj. Rogers can furnish, the whole commanded by Maj. Campbell, to march tomorrow two hours before daybreak by the same route Col. Haviland took; which post Capt. Johnson will show, and to remain there whilst the boats are fishing. They are to take one day's provisions and to go as light as possible as they are not only a covering party to the boats, but to attack any body of the enemy they may find.

Lake George, 5th July, 1759

A General Court Martial to set tomorrow morning at the President's Tent at 8 o'clock for the trial of a man suspected of robbery. . . . Major Graham and two captains of the Royal Highlanders to attend.

LAKE GEORGE 8TH JULY, 1759

The Royal Highlanders will take the Gen's Guard tomorrow half an hour after 4.

LAKE GEORGE, 11TH JULY, 1759

Capt. John Campbell of the Royal Highlanders is appointed Major in the late Forbes, and is to be obeyed as such. Royal Highlanders to receive 35 *batteaux*. Oars and whatever else belongs to the *batteaux* will be delivered at the same time. Each *batteaux* will carry 12 barrels of flour or 9 of pork when ordered to load, and it is supposed will have about 20 men or a few more in each *batteaux*.

LAKE GEORGE, 12TH JULY, 1759

A General Court Martial of the Regulars to be held tomorrow morning at 6 o'clock. Col. Grant President, Major John Campbell to attend.

LAKE GEORGE, 13TH JULY, 1759

Colonel of the Day tomorrow, Col. Grant. Field Officer tomorrow night, Major Graham. General's Guard tomorrow, Royal Highlanders. The General Court Martial of which Col. Grant was President, is dissolved. Royal Highlanders to receive a proportion of flour for five days which they are to get baked tomorrow and keep.

Lake George, 19th July, 1759

The Royal Highlanders one of the Regiments appointed to sit in general Court Martial tomorrow at 6 o'clock. The Regiments to load their *batteaux* tomorrow morning beginning at 5 o'clock in the following manner, Montgomery's Pork, Royal Highlanders, Flour. . . . two regiments to load at a time, one flour and one pork, and to be allowed an hour for loading, and when loaded to return to their stations.

Lake George, 20th July, 1759

For the day this day, Regulars, Col. Grant. On landing the Col. Grant to take the command of the late Forbes' Brigade.

Camp near Ticonderoga, 22nd July

For the piquet tomorrow night, Major Graham.

Camp before Ticonderoga, 23rd July, 1759

Col. of the day tomorrow, Col. Grant. Field Officer of the piquets this night, Major Graham.

Camp at Ticonderoga, 24th July, 1759

Sergt. Murray of the Royal Highland Regiment is appointed to oversee people making fascines, and to keep an account of the number made.

Camp at Ticonderoga, 25th July, 1759

The following carpenters. . . . James Frazer, George McDougall, James Frazer, John McColme, John Robinson, James Gumming, and James McDonald of the Royal Highlanders to be at the sawmills tomorrow at 5 o'clock and if Capt. Loreing should not be there they will receive their directions from Brigadier Ruggles.

The Royal Highland Regiment to draw tomorrow early two days biscuits and two days pork, biscuits in lieu of flour, which completes them to the 28th inclusive.

Ticonderoga, 26th July, 1759

Adjutant for the day tomorrow Royal Highlands.

Ticonderoga, 28th July, 1759

A General Court Martial of the line to be held at the President's tent at 8 o'clock tomorrow morning. Col. Grant, President, two Majors and ten Captains, two of whom are from the Royal Highlanders.

Ticonderoga, 29th July, 1759

The ovens to be given for the use of troops in the following manner: . . . . No. 2 to the Inniskilling and Royal Highlanders. No bakers but such as those Corps employ to make in any of those ovens. The Royal Highland Regiments to strike their tents and march immediately to the Landing Place, and they will send their tents and baggage in *batteaux*.

TICONDEROGA, 1ST AUGUST, 1759

As a number of shoes are come up, intended for the use of the Army, and will be delivered to them at the prime cost in England, which three shillings and six pence per pair. The Regiments may receive in the following manner and proportion, or as many of that proportion as they like to take by applying to Mr. Tucker, agent to Mr. Kilby at the Landing Place. Royal Highlanders 366.

Capt. Reid is appointed Major to the Royal Highland Regiment.

CROWN POINT, 5TH AUGUST, 1759

Col. of the day tomorrow Regulars Col. Grant; Field officer for the piquet tomorrow night Maj. Reid.

CROWN POINT, 6TH AUGUST, 1759

Adjutant of the day tomorrow Royal Highlanders. As twenty-four barrels of Spruce beer is come to the fort the corps may send for it immediately in the following proportions. . . . Royal Highlanders, three barrels.

CROWN POINT, 7TH AUGUST, 1759

Corporal Sinclair of the Highlanders and Parceloo of the Inniskilling Regiment with 16 labourers used to digging to attend Lieut. Gray Tomorrow at 5 o'clock; the evening gun is the signal for the working party to leave off work.

CROWN POINT, 8TH AUGUST, 1759

The Regulars to receive 4 days provisions tomorrow of pork, beginning at Reveille Beating by Forbes followed by Royal Highlanders, etc. It is concluded that they have their bread from Ticonderoga as was ordered.

CROWN POINT, 10TH AUGUST, 1759

Ens. Gregor of the Royal Highlanders. . . . are appointed overseers of the works that are carrying on at the fort. They will attend Lieut. Col. Eyre tomorrow morning at 5 o'clock and follow such directions as they shall receive from him.

CROWN POINT, 11TH AUGUST, 1759

Col. of the day tomorrow, Col. Grant. For the building of the fort the following quarries. . . . five of the Royal Highlanders. . . . to attend Lieut. Col. Eyre tomorrow morning at the hour of work, and are to continue daily to work as quarriers.

CROWN POINT, 12TH AUGUST, 1759

Adjutant of the Day tomorrow, Royal Highlanders.

CROWN POINT, 14TH AUGUST, 1759

Field officer for the work tomorrow, Major Reid.

CROWN POINT, 15TH AUGUST. 1759

The following Surgeons Mates are to join the Regiments and serve as Mates in room of Officers serving as such; Mr. Goldthwat an additional Mate in the Royal Highlanders to be put on the establishment of Forbe's, Mr. Carter to the Royal Highlanders.

CROWN POINT, 16TH AUGUST, 1759

The following sawyers are to attend Lieut. Col. Eyre tomorrow at 5 o'clock:. . . . Royal Highlanders, Robert Kennedy, John McFarling and Robert Bain. The following masons are likewise to attend Lieut. Col. Eyre tomorrow morning at 5 o'clock:. . . . Royal Highlanders, Dougal McKeafter and John Stewart. The above artificers are to work daily and to follow such directions as they shall receive from Lieut. Col. Eyre.

CROWN POINT, 17TH AUGUST, 1759

Col. of the day tomorrow, Col. Grant.

The following masons to attend Lieut. Col. Eyre tomorrow morning at five o'clock:.... Royal Highlanders Angus McDonald and William Milligan.

CROWN POINT, 18TH AUGUST, 1759

Adjutant of the day tomorrow, Royal Highlanders.

CROWN POINT, 24TH AUG., 1759

Adjutant of the day, tomorrow, Royal Highlanders.

CROWN POINT, 27TH AUGUST, 1759

The following soldiers to attend Lieut. Eyre tomorrow morning at 5 o'clock and to take their directions from him; Royal Highlanders, John Fraser, John McElvore, James Bruce, Allex'r Sutherland.

CROWN POINT, 28TH AUGUST, 1759

Field Officer of the work tomorrow Major Reid.

CROWN POINT, 30TH AUGUST, 1759

Adjutant of the day, Royal Highlanders.

CROWN POINT, 1ST SEPTEMBER, 1759

Col. of the day, tomorrow, Col. Grant.

CROWN POINT, 3RD SEPTEMBER, 1759

John McNeal, Grenadier in Royal Highland
Regiment. . . . to attend Lieut. Col. Eyre this
day at 12 o'clock and to follow such directions
as he shall give.

CROWN POINT, 4TH SEPTEMBER, 1759

Col. of the day, tomorrow, Col. Grant.

Field Officer for the work, Major Reid.

The men of the Royal Highland Regiment who
have been employed in making baskets will
be paid for the same by the Quartermaster's
applying to Mr. Gray this afternoon after
the work is over. The Regiments to receive
tomorrow morning two pounds of fresh meat
and one pound of rice for the number of men
set opposite the names of each corps, and the
Regiments are to apply said fresh beef and
rice entirely for the use of the sick. Royal
Highlanders 22.

CROWN POINT, 5TH SEPTEMBER, 1759

Field Officer for the works tomorrow, Major Reid.

Adjutant of the day, tomorrow, Royal Highlanders.

The Black Watch in the 1759 Campaign

Allex'r Forbes of the Royal Highlanders, mason,
to accompany Lieut. Col. Eyre tomorrow and
follow such directions as he shall give.

Crown Point, 6th September, 1759

Sergt. Clark of the Royal Highlanders to be one of
the four sergeants to attend the works daily and
to receive directions from Lieut. Col. Eyre.

Crown Point, 7th September, 1759

For the day, tomorrow, Col. Grant.

Crown Point, 11th September, 1759

Adjutant of the day tomorrow, Royal Highlanders.
A general court martial of the Regulars to sit
tomorrow at the President's Tent at 8 o'clock;
Col. Foster, President, Major John Campbell,
Major Reid. . . . one captain of the Royal
Highlanders.

Crown Point, 12th September, 1759

A detachment of 100 Grenadiers, 30 of the Light
Infantry of Regiments, non-commissioned
officers in proportion to be commanded by a
captain of the Grenadiers and 2 Subalterns of
each Corps to parade tomorrow at Reveille
beating on the left of the front of the light
infantry and to take 30 *batteaux* to Ticonderoga

where he is to apply to the Commissary and load 15 with 30 barrels of flour in each *batteaux*, the other 15 with 16 barrels of pork each. The Royal Highland Regiment to furnish the *batteaux* and the captain commanding the party will see them this night that they may be ready to set off at Reveille beating and to return as soon as they are loaded.

CROWN POINT, 15TH SEPTEMBER, 1759

For the day tomorrow, Col. Grant.

Field Officer for the piquets this night, Regulars Major Reid.

Field Officer for the works tomorrow, Major John Campbell.

CROWN POINT, 16TH SEPTEMBER, 1759

Field Officer for the works tomorrow, Major Reid.

CROWN POINT, 17TH SEPTEMBER

Adjutant of the day tomorrow, Royal Highlanders.

CROWN POINT, 18TH SEPTEMBER, 1759

For the day tomorrow, Col. Grant.

CROWN POINT, 21ST SEPTEMBER, 1759

For the day tomorrow, Col. Grant.

For the piquets this night, Major Reid.

Field Officer for the works tomorrow, Major John Campbell.

CROWN POINT, 23RD SEPTEMBER, 1759

Adjutant of the day tomorrow, Royal Highlanders.

CROWN POINT, 25TH SEPTEMBER, 1759

Lieut. Tolmey of the Royal Highlanders is appointed Overseer for the work on the fort and to receive his directions from Leiut. Col. Eyre.

CROWN POINT, 26TH SEPTEMBER, 1759

Field officer for the piquets this night, Major John Campbell; tomorrow night, Major Reid.

CROWN POINT, 27TH SEPTEMBER, 1759

For the day tomorrow, Col. Grant.

Field Officer for the piquets this night, Major Reid.

CROWN POINT, 29TH SEPTEMBER, 1759

Adjutant for the day tomorrow, Royal Highlanders.

CROWN POINT, 30TH SEPTEMBER, 1759

Col. for the day tomorrow, Col. Grant.

CROWN POINT, 2ND OCTOBER, 1759

Field Officer for the Picquits this night, Major John Campbell; tomorrow night, Major Reid.

CROWN POINT, 3RD OCTOBER, 1759

For the day tomorrow, Col. Grant.
Field Officer for the piquets this night, Major Reid.
Field Officer for the works tomorrow, John Campbell.
A General Court martial of the Regulars to sit at the President's tent tomorrow at 9 o'clock. . . . two captains of the Royal Highlanders.

CROWN POINT, 5TH OCTOBER, 1759

Adjutant of the day tomorrow, Royal Highlanders.

CROWN POINT, 6TH OCTOBER, 1759

For the day tomorrow, Col. Grant.
The regular regiments to give in their cartridges that are damaged this day to the artillery and to receive as much powder, paper, ball and twine as will complete their ammunition. The Royal Highlanders 475.

CROWN POINT, 7TH OCTOBER, 1759

The Regiments to prepare their *batteaux* to the following numbers and to have their sails fixed

according to pattern Col. Haviland approved of. . . .
Royal Highlanders 24. . . .

CROWN POINT, 8TH OCTOBER, 1759

Royal Highlanders are to take two *batteaux* more
than what were ordered yesterday.

CROWN POINT, 9TH OCTOBER, 1759

For the day tomorrow, Col. Grant.

Field Officer for piquets this night, Major Reid.

The under mentioned Corps are to send a *batteaux*
each at Retreat beating to Ticonderoga to
receive tomorrow morning the following
number of loaves weighing six pounds and a half
each; they are to pay to the person Gen. Lyman
appoints to receive the money the following
sums being one penny sterling for baking seven
pounds of flour: Royal Highlanders 460 loaves,
£1. 7. 8d Sterling. . . .

The Royal Highlanders are to leave Subaltern
Officer each, exclusive of officers employed
as overseers at the King's Works, with three
Sergeants, three Corp'ls each with the men that
are left behind; when the Regiments march, the
officers and men of each corps will encamp on
the centre of the encampment of the Corps. . . .
and a sentry to be kept in the encampment that
nothing may be spoiled or taken away during the
absence of the Regiment. The Regiments are

to give the following numbers for the Brig and Sloop and will send seamen if they have them: for the Brig. . . . Royal Highlanders 14 men.

CROWN POINT, 11TH OCTOBER, 1759

Adjutant of the day tomorrow, Royal Highlanders.

LAKE CHAMPLAINE, 15TH OCTOBER, 1759

For the day tomorrow, Col. Grant.

LIGONIER BAY, 14TH OCTOBER, 1759

Field Officer for the piquet this night, Major John Campbell; tomorrow night, Major Reid.

LAKE CHAMPLAINE, 15TH OCTOBER, 1759

For the day tomorrow, Col. Grant.
Field Officer for the piquets this night, Major Reid.

CAMP AT SCHUYLERS ISLAND, 18TH OCTOBER, 1759

For the day tomorrow, Col. Grant.

CROWN POINT, 22ND OCTOBER, 1759

Adjutant of the day tomorrow, Royal Highlanders.

CROWN POINT, 25TH OCTOBER, 1759

22 men of the Royal Highlanders are to be sent to the Hospital at Fort Edward. . . . The surgeon of the Royal Highlanders is to attend them to Fort Edward, a Corporal and 6 men of the Royal Highlanders with one *bateaux*. . . . are to convey the sick to the Sawmills, where the officer will leave the *batteau* with Lieut. Col. Miller and march the sick to the Landing Place.

CROWN POINT, 27TH OCTOBER, 1759

For the day tomorrow, Col. Grant.
Field Officer for the piquets this night, Major Reid.

CROWN POINT, 28TH OCTOBER, 1759

Adjutant for the day tomorrow, Royal Highlanders.

CROWN POINT, 30TH OCTOBER, 1759

Officer for the day, tomorrow, Col. Grant.
A General Court martial to be held at the President's Tent tomorrow at 9 o'clock to try all such prisoners as shall be brought before them; Col. Grant, President. . . . One Captain of the Royal Highlanders.

CROWN POINT, 31ST OCTOBER, 1759

Field Officer for the piquets this night, Major Reid.

The General Court martial of which Col. Grant was President is dissolved; the Prisoners of the Royal Highland Regiment is acquitted.

CROWN POINT, 1ST NOVEMBER, 1759

For the day tomorrow, Col. Grant.

CROWN POINT, 3RD NOVEMBER, 1759

For the piquets tomorrow night, Major John Campbell.

For the works tomorrow, Major John Campbell.

Adjutant of the day tomorrow, Royal Highlanders.

ALSO FROM LEONAUR

AVAILABLE IN SOFTCOVER OR HARDCOVER WITH DUST JACKET

SEPOYS, SIEGE & STORM by *Charles John Griffiths*—The Experiences of a young officer of H.M.'s 61st Regiment at Ferozepore, Delhi ridge and at the fall of Delhi during the Indian mutiny 1857.

CAMPAIGNING IN ZULULAND by *W. E. Montague*—Experiences on campaign during the Zulu war of 1879 with the 94th Regiment.

THE STORY OF THE GUIDES by *G. J. Younghusband*—The Exploits of the Soldiers of the famous Indian Army Regiment from the northwest frontier 1847 - 1900..

ZULU: 1879 by *D.C.F. Moodie & the Leonaur Editors*—The Anglo-Zulu War of 1879 from contemporary sources: First Hand Accounts, Interviews, Dispatches, Official Documents & Newspaper Reports.

THE RECOLLECTIONS OF SKINNER OF SKINNER'S HORSE by *James Skinner*—James Skinner and his 'Yellow Boys' Irregular cavalry in the wars of India between the British, Mahratta, Rajput, Mogul, Sikh & Pindarree Forces.

TOMMY ATKINS' WAR STORIES 14 FIRST HAND ACCOUNTS—Fourteen first hand accounts from the ranks of the British Army during Queen Victoria's Empire Original & True Battle Stories Recollections of the Indian Mutiny With the 49th in the Crimea With the Guards in Egypt The Charge of the Six Hundred With Wolseley in Ashanti Alma, Inkermann and Magdala With the Gunners at Tel-el-Kebir Russian Guns and Indian Rebels Rough Work in the Crimea In the Maori Rising Facing the Zulus From Sebastopol to Lucknow Sent to Save Gordon On the March to Chitral Tommy by Rudyard Kipling

CHASSEUR OF 1914 by *Marcel Dupont*—Experiences of the twilight of the French Light Cavalry by a young officer during the early battles of the great war in Europe.

TROOP HORSE & TRENCH by *R. A. Lloyd*—The experiences of a British Lifeguardsman of the household cavalry fighting on the western front during the First World War 1914-18.

THE EAST AFRICAN MOUNTED RIFLES by *C. J. Wilson*—Experiences of the campaign in the East African bush during the First World War.

THE FIGHTING CAMELIERS by *Frank Reid*—The exploits of the Imperial Camel Corps in the desert and Palestine campaigns of the First World War.

LEONAUR

ALSO FROM LEONAUR
AVAILABLE IN SOFTCOVER OR HARDCOVER WITH DUST JACKET

THE COMPLEAT RIFLEMAN HARRIS *by Benjamin Harris as told to & transcribed by Captain Henry Curling*—The adventures of a soldier of the 95th (Rifles) during the Peninsular Campaign of the Napoleonic Wars

WITH WELLINGTON'S LIGHT CAVALRY *by William Tomkinson*—The Experiences of an officer of the 16th Light Dragoons in the Peninsular and Waterloo campaigns of the Napoleonic Wars.

SERGEANT BOURGOGNE *by Adrien Bourgogne*—With Napoleon's Imperial Guard in the Russian Campaign and on the Retreat from Moscow 1812 - 13.

SWORDS OF HONOUR *by Henry Newbolt & Stanley L. Wood*—The Careers of Six Outstanding Officers from the Napoleonic Wars, the Wars for India and the American Civil War, with dozens of illustrations by Stanley L. Wood.

SURTEES OF THE RIFLES *by William Surtees*—A Soldier of the 95th (Rifles) in the Peninsular campaign of the Napoleonic Wars.

ENSIGN BELL IN THE PENINSULAR WAR *by George Bell*—The Experiences of a young British Soldier of the 34th Regiment 'The Cumberland Gentlemen' in the Napoleonic wars.

HUSSAR IN WINTER *by Alexander Gordon*—A British Cavalry Officer during the retreat to Corunna in the Peninsular campaign of the Napoleonic Wars.

NAPOLEONIC WAR STORIES *by Sir Arthur Quiller-Couch*—Tales of soldiers, spies, battles & sieges from the Peninsular & Waterloo campaingns.

JOURNALS OF ROBERT ROGERS OF THE RANGERS *by Robert Rogers*—The exploits of Rogers & the Rangers in his own words during 1755-1761 in the French & Indian War.

KERSHAW'S BRIGADE VOLUME 1 *by D. Augustus Dickert*—Manassas, Seven Pines, Sharpsburg (Antietam), Fredricksburg, Chancellorsville, Gettysburg, Chickamauga, Chattanooga, Fort Sanders & Bean Station..

KERSHAW'S BRIGADE VOLUME 2 *by D. Augustus Dickert*—At the wilderness, Cold Harbour, Petersburg, The Shenandoah Valley and Cedar Creek.

A TIGER ON HORSEBACK *by L. March Phillips*—The Experiences of a Trooper & Officer of Rimington's Guides - The Tigers - during the Anglo-Boer war 1899 - 1902.

Printed in the United Kingdom
by Lightning Source UK Ltd.
122803UK00002B/604/A